# Get Mears!
## Frederick Mears: Builder of the Alaska Railroad

Colonel Frederick Mears

# Get Mears!

## Frederick Mears: Builder of the Alaska Railroad

*Katharine Carson Crittenden*

**Binford & Mort Publishing**
Portland, Oregon

in cooperation with
**Cook Inlet Historical Society**
Anchorage, Alaska

Drawings by Edwin Crittenden
Maps by Karen Crittenden

*Get Mears!*
*Frederick Mears: Builder of the Alaska Railroad*

Copyright © 2002 by Binford & Mort Publishing

Printed in the United States of America

Library of Congress Catalog Card Number: 200197541

ISBN 0-8323-0550-2
ISBN 0-8323-0551-0 pbk

First Edition 2002

FREDERICK MEARS
1878 – 1939

# CONTENTS

# PREFACE

*It has been said that every great achievement is but
the shadow of a man. If so, it must in justice be
said that the Alaska Railroad is the shadow of an
intrepid builder, once a lieutenant of cavalry, later
a colonel of engineers overseas, whose construction,
like his character and conception of service, was
without flaw.*

These words were spoken in 1923 by Secretary of Interior
Hubert Work on the occasion of the driving of the golden spike
which signaled completion of the 470-mile government railroad in
Alaska. The man he praised was Colonel Frederick Mears, who since
1914 had served as chief engineer for construction of the railroad
from the tidewaters of the Pacific to the interior of Alaska. President Warren Harding, his staff, their wives, and numerous other
prominent officials had traveled north for the ceremony. The historic event made news worldwide.

Conspicuously absent from among the dignitaries was the one
who deserved the major honors: Colonel Mears had not been in-

vited to participate. To this day, his name is seldom recognized. Most Alaskans are unaware that an inscription to him was engraved on the celebrated golden spike and that the spike had earlier been given to Mears by the people of Anchorage, who considered him their guiding light. A plaque on the Tanana River bridge and surviving structures at Dutch Harbor are the only remaining public commemoratives of his service in Alaska.

The striking personage of Frederick Mears first caught my attention when I served as chairman of the Anchorage Historical Landmarks Preservation Commission in the late 1970s. One of our goals was to preserve as many as possible of the fine houses built in Anchorage during construction of the Alaska Railroad. While exploring the railroad archives, I learned how Anchorage came into being and who its champions and detractors were. From this investigation, it was evident that Colonel Mears, as chief engineer of the Alaska Engineering Commission and later as chairman, had also played a vital role in fostering the town's early growth. Intrigued, I determined to find out more about this man—who he was, where he came from, and how it happened that President Woodrow Wilson chose him to engineer one of the largest transportation projects of the century. The search took me from Alaska through the Cascade Mountains, to Montana's Glacier Park, to the battlefield of Custer's last stand, to old forts of the west, and to the Panama Canal. I pored through old newspapers, government and military documents, books, speeches, and letters, and I met and corresponded with members of the Mears family.

From this series of inquiries, I came to the realization that Colonel Mears had received less than his share of credit for the engineering projects he had completed in his lifetime. An important page in the history of Alaska, and indeed in that of the United States, was missing. This book is a first step toward filling that void and reclaiming the lost history.

Frederick Mears' life story offers a new perspective about a time when the nation was overwhelmed with a paranoia that plagued its well-being and political health. It reveals the arbitrary way in which world events can alter the course of one person's life. In paying tribute to Colonel Mears, this account of his legacy will acquaint readers with the man and his accomplishments, which were pivotal to railroad history in Panama, France, the Pacific Northwest, and Alaska.

# INTRODUCTION

The United States purchased the territory of Alaska from Russia in 1867, just eleven years before the birth of Frederick Mears. Development in Alaska languished for a lengthy period following the transfer, as the United States discovered why Russia had experienced defeat and frustration in attempting to pry open the northern domain. Closed off by impenetrable mountain ranges and located 4,000 miles from the seat of government, Alaska presented a challenge of immense proportions. Compounding the difficulties was the fact that most Americans considered Alaska to be a frozen wasteland and its acquisition a folly. Even though the federal government's revenue from early fur-seal trade alone nearly equaled the $7.2 million it had paid for the territory, legislators repeatedly questioned its worth.

When prospectors struck gold in the 1890s, Alaska took on new importance. Geological explorations by the government had confirmed that, in addition to offering plentiful quantities of fish and timber, the land contained large deposits of valuable minerals and coal. Eventually, Congress came to the realization that orderly development of the territory and its riches would depend on establishing a system of public transportation. A railroad from the Pacific coast to the interior of Alaska seemed the most expedient means of gaining access to the vast resources there.

The general area occupied today by the city of Anchorage was virtually uninhabited in 1915, when it was chosen to serve as headquarters for the terminal operations of the government's railroad to the interior. Situated near the headwaters of Cook Inlet on

Alaska's southcentral coast, and ringed on three sides by mountains, the setting is spectacular. To the east and south stands the Chugach Range, and to the north rises the Alaska Range, culminating in North America's largest massif, Mount McKinley. Dwarfed by nature's majesty, the camp of white tents set up for railroad workers was an inglorious beginning for the city that is now the largest in Alaska.

In the decades following its incorporation in 1920, Anchorage remained a small town, extending approximately ten blocks in any direction. The establishment of two large military bases nearby during World War II did little to alter that configuration. Statehood in 1958 brought change, but discovery of oil at Prudhoe Bay ten years later, and a hundred years after the purchase of Alaska, prompted major growth. When oil revenues began accruing to the state, beautiful new civic and office buildings, schools, hospitals, and hotels emerged to transform the city's landscape.

Although Anchorage today is endowed with magnificent surroundings and a colorful past, its inception as a railroad construction camp on the mud flats of Ship Creek has seldom been promoted as part of its history. Developers and historians alike have chosen instead to emphasize the area's connection with English explorer Captain James Cook, who in 1778 sailed into Cook Inlet looking for the elusive Northwest Passage. While that event deserves recognition, it should not be confused with the city's true origin.

Frederick Mears was a man whose destiny became inextricably linked to the founding of Anchorage and to the history of the 49th state. He was the engineer who built the government railroad on the last frontier, the army colonel who drove the wedge that opened up Alaska. What follows is the story of his life.

## CHAPTER 1

# THE RIGHT MAN FOR ALASKA

*Alaska is our greatest asset....Guard it well, do not let it lie dormant when the Panama Canal is about to open. This railroad means that Alaska shall be made prosperous to take its place as our sentinel and our key to the new Pacific.*

Albert Johnson, Washington
State Congressman, 1914

The year was 1914, and America's newly-elected president, Woodrow Wilson, faced a tough decision. Congress had just authorized $35 million to build a trunk line of railroad in the territory of Alaska. One of Wilson's goals as president was to open up the territory for the "service and development of the country and its people." Now, at last, he had the go-ahead to make it happen, but who should manage the project?

Surrounded by the tranquil, refined environs of the nation's capital that March, Wilson could only vaguely envision how such an enterprise might actually be accomplished. Crossing those vast stretches of wilderness far to the north was going to be a project almost equal in scope to the building of the Panama Canal. Critics of the idea were loudly questioning its feasibility, especially considering the nature of Alaska's terrain and its short construction season. At the same time, supporters were adamant about the urgency to proceed.

Few stipulations were placed upon the expenditure of the appropriation or the creation of an agency to direct the work. After considerable deliberation, Wilson and his chief advisor in the matter, Secretary of Interior Franklin Lane, decided to appoint a three-member board to manage the operation in Alaska. One of the three would need to have experience in building railroads on the frontier, one must know the territory, and one must be skilled at engineering large-scale projects—preferably an army engineer. Their top candidate for the army engineering position was Colonel George W. Goethals, a hydraulics engineer of renown and sometimes referred to as the "genius" of the Panama Canal. An officer of the Army Corps of Engineers, Goethals had been appointed chief engineer of the canal project in 1907 by President Theodore Roosevelt.

Secretary Lane thought Goethals would be perfect for the Alaska assignment. He soon learned, however, that the man planned to retire upon completion of the canal and the closing of his term as governor of Panama. Even so, Lane, who had just finished his own tenure as chairman of the Interstate Commerce Commission, was eager to put into motion his far-reaching ideas about how to best develop Alaska. He wasn't in the habit of wasting time.

The Panama Canal had taken more than a decade to complete—triple that, counting the earlier efforts by the French. No one knew at this point how many years of construction the railroad in Alaska might require. Consequently, it would seem right to look for someone much younger than Goethals for the appointment. The best compromise, Lane reasoned, would be an army engineer with experience under Goethals in Panama. The mission now was to find that man.

The answer came when Wilson summoned Goethals to the White House for a consultation. Still energetic at sixty, military in carriage with a healthy shock of white hair, Goethals nodded in agreement to Lane's spirited portrayal of the job to be done: making surveys, formulating designs, assembling supplies and materials, hiring workers, overseeing construction, writing reports, keeping budgets, contending with rugged terrain, and surviving harsh weather. Upon hearing all of the qualifications required of the candidate, Goethals said without reservation, "Get Mears!"

There was no question in his mind who would be best suited for the position Secretary Lane was describing. Army lieutenant Frederick Mears had repeatedly proven his abilities during the seven years he had worked for Goethals—beginning on the Panama Railroad, then with other major construction projects on the Isthmus, and most recently with the steamship company's operations there. Certainly, he was prepared for the intellectual and physical aspects of the Alaska work. Still, the continuing political debate over the railroad in the territory might create obstacles of a different nature. Goethals could only express confidence that Mears would be able to overcome whatever difficulties arose in Alaska, just as he had done when the going got rough in Panama.

Physically, Mears was a picture of the American pioneering engineer. At thirty-six, he appeared lean, wiry and bronzed, with a gleam of red in his hair and a hint of freckles across his face. A check into his background would leave no doubt that Colonel Goethals had good reason to recommend him for the Alaska appointment. Son of a Civil War veteran, Mears had a brilliant service record of his own, and the military had trained him in civil engineering. By all accounts, he was a man of ambition and integrity, who followed a strong work ethic. These were traits he acquired through the example of his father, Lieutenant Colonel Frederick J. Mears, an accomplished horseman with a long and varied army career.


## BORN OF THE ARMY

At the start of the Civil War, Frederick's father had closed his law practice in Chicago to enlist, without fee or compensation, in the citizens' militia for the District of Columbia. In April 1861, at the age of twenty-four, he joined the Regular Army, drilling thousands of recruits and serving alternately with the New York Volunteer Sharpshooters for brief periods. Then he was stationed at Vancouver Barracks in Washington Territory as an aide to the commander of the Department of the Columbia. Although his duty there was short, the senior Mears endeavored to improve the health and morale of the men by directing the repair of the damp, run-down log buildings at the post and by overseeing the planting of a vegetable garden before he left.

Elizabeth Morse McFarland came into his life while he was stationed at Point San Jose, California, in the final months of the Civil War. Just nineteen when she met him, Elizabeth had recently arrived in San Francisco from Bangor, Maine. Before long, the two were seriously interested in one another, though he was nearly ten years her senior. By June of 1865, the army had subdued the unrest that broke out in San Francisco following the assassination of President Lincoln. This reprieve enabled Mears to take personal leave to be married. The couple's Episcopal ceremony was performed in Acapulco, Mexico, at the home of the U.S. consul. Elizabeth, however, was not ready to embrace the nomadic life of the military, nor the lonely waiting at the post for her husband's return. She chose instead to remain in San Francisco and to reunite with him whenever possible.

Lieutenant Colonel Frederick J. Mears, father.

*Mears collection*

Elizabeth Morse MacFarland Mears, mother.

## LIFE AT OMAHA BARRACKS

For ten years during the Indian campaigns, the senior Mears was rotated between army posts in the Dakotas, Washington Territory, Wyoming, Idaho, Oregon, California, Nevada and Nebraska. According to family legend, his regiment barely escaped annihilation in 1876, when General George Armstrong Custer charged into the conflict at Little Bighorn.

While stationed at Omaha Barracks, Nebraska, he wrote to Elizabeth of the comfortable home she would enjoy as the wife of an officer, if only he could induce her to join him there. Wide verandas fronted all of the residences, which were heated by coal and wood-burning stoves. Coal-oil lamps provided light. Tall, double-hung windows throughout the buildings offered fine views of the tree-lined parade ground and the Missouri River two miles distant. By now, the couple had two small children who were nearly old enough to travel—a son, Ned, and a daughter, Winifred. So, in due time, Elizabeth decided to move the family to Nebraska.

Traveling by train across the dry and desolate plains country, the young mother saw the lush California greenery, acacia, and palm trees slowly fade from view. Western in the worst sense of the word, the city of Omaha in the late 1870s had only one edifice, the Omaha Stock Exchange. Plaided in squares of red, white, and blue, it bore a stark contrast to the elegant facades of San Francisco.

For Elizabeth, not just the scenery but her entire way of life would change on the military outpost. Wanting to add a sense of refinement and permanence to the otherwise austere quarters, she had filled her round-topped trunks with her best linens and quilts, family portraits, china, and a few pieces of wedding silver. She had also brought along books, games, her treadle sewing machine, a wind-up Victrola, and a baby's cradle.

The army post was comparable to any small town of the period, standing alone on an 80-acre plateau of rich, black earth four miles northeast of the city. It had its own school, guardhouse, blacksmith shop, bakery, laundry, mess hall and administrative offices—

about forty buildings in all. This was also the place where companies of cavalry assembled to protect mail-carrying stage coaches and pioneers migrating west. Hundreds of horses and mules were stabled there.

When winter approached in 1877, and snow and cold enveloped the post, Elizabeth found she had to rely on her own resources in her husband's absence. To pass the long hours she endeared herself to her children by recounting stories of their relatives from ages past. Her dark eyes brightened when she told about her McFarland forefathers in southern Scotland. She assured the children that someday, if they were fortunate enough to travel, they would be able to see their ancestral home on beautiful Loch Lomand. Upon learning that Samuel Morse, inventor of the telegraph, was another one of their relatives, the children immediately wanted to send a wire to grandfather McFarland in San Francisco. And, whenever Elizabeth retold the story of their father's relationship to Robert de la Mere, a cousin of William the Conqueror, it always led to a long and colorful account of the Normans and their fearless adventures.

With the onset of spring, the Mearses eagerly awaited the birth of another child. The year was 1878, the same year American poet Carl Sandburg was born, the year of the second Exhibition Universelle in Paris, the year Gilbert and Sullivan's *HMS Pinafore* was first performed and electric street lighting was introduced in London. The boy arrived May 25, at Omaha Barracks hospital. They named him Frederick after his father. This son would spend virtually all of his formative years immersed in army life.

As a youngster, curly-haired Freddy awakened to the morning gun and the sounds of reveille. Each day, bugles summoned troops for school, guard mount, and dressage movements, and called them to their quarters in the evening. It was like watching a passing parade. Yet, as he soon learned, those routines were important because they helped each soldier remember his position and be ready to follow commands in times of battle.

*Mears collection*

Young Frederick, left, and brother, Ned.

The boy was initiated early into the life of the soldier-horse-man. He thrilled at the spectacle of army men charging on their steeds across the countryside and clearing the worst obstacles with ease. At the same time, he began to comprehend his father's dedi-cation and bravery for traveling hundreds of miles on horseback through the semi-arid regions of the west and returning weeks later, dusty and unshaven with his uniform in tatters. Those were emo-tionally distressing times for his mother, and as Frederick grew older he understood why. Whenever Elizabeth's husband left, her eyes would fill with tears as she reminded her children to say good-bye and turn their backs. It was the custom, she said, never to watch the column out of sight because so many soldiers never returned.

## AMBITION AND EDUCATION TO MATCH

When Frederick was nine years old he attended public school in New York City. His father had moved the family there on a two-year appointment as commander of the David's Island Recruit-ing Center. Having been raised in the big city, the elder Mears looked forward to sharing with the children his memories of what the place looked like when he was a boy. There was no Statue of Liberty then, and the Brooklyn Bridge had not yet been built. He described teams of horses pulling omnibuses full of passengers over bumpy cobblestone streets—an excursion young Frederick surely would have enjoyed.

For a child raised in the west, the sights and sounds of the harbor enveloped in fog must have been spellbinding. Watching enormous ships set sail for foreign destinations would spark the imagination of any young boy. In another few years, Frederick him-self would step aboard such a vessel here for the first of many ocean voyages of his own.

In 1888, the senior Mears was detailed at Fort Sherman, Idaho. A year later, he was ordered to proceed with his regiment to Fort

*Frank Palmer photo, courtesy Spokane Public Library/Northwest Room*

Old Fort Spokane, Washington, where Frederick Mears lived with his parents and family as a youth.

Spokane, Washington, where Frederick continued his schooling in the nearby town of Spokane Falls, as it was then known. By now, the Mearses were able to enjoy the colorful activities frequently offered on the post. Soldiers stationed there in those years spent most of their time training for battles that never occurred. On only a few occasions were they called out to demonstrate their presence to the local Salish. But not a single shot was ever fired.

No doubt the veteran soldier found life a bit dull as commander of this fortification, after the action-packed life of his earlier years. He suffered an unheralded death that followed a bad fall on the icy steps of his home in January 1892. By that time he had achieved the rank of lieutenant colonel, Fourth Infantry, and held the Bronze Cross for loyal and faithful service. He was fifty-six years old when his thirty-one-year military career came to an end.

Elizabeth was in no way prepared for her husband's sudden death. Had he perished in battle, the shock might have been less devastating, but this time there had been no forewarning. At forty-six, she was enjoying her life as the wife of a respected army officer and the well-deserved leisure they shared. She remained in Spokane, while Frederick completed the academic studies at Gonzaga Preparatory School, but then moved back to California.

Frederick's mother and father were caring, disciplined parents. They never promised that life would be easy. Peering forth from their sepia-toned portraits, they seemed to counsel him, "Life's demands will always be there, but we carried on and you will too."

## BROADENING HORIZONS

At this point in his life, Frederick, then fifteen, enrolled at Shattuck Military Academy, the same institution his father had attended. Located near the industrial center of Faribault, Minnesota, Shattuck was fifty miles south of St. Paul and Minneapolis. The

*Mears collection*

Frederick Mears graduated from Shattuck Military Academy in 1897.

school followed the academic model of West Point and offered a
military training program. Students were required to take Greek,
Latin, civil government, trigonometry, qualitative analysis, and mechanical drawing, in addition to the basic courses.

Though nostalgic for his father at first, Frederick found the
years at Shattuck to be happy ones. He excelled in his studies as
well as in military performance. At the opening of his senior term,
he was appointed a company commander in the school's corps of
cadets. By then, the sandy haired young man had attained the height
of six feet.

Summer work was easy to find, since everything from woolen
goods, shoes, and tools to elevators, automobiles, and furniture
was manufactured in the area. After earning his first wage, Frederick proudly sent it to his mother. When possible, he visited her
and Winifred in San Francisco, and occasionally he went to see
Ned and his friends in Oregon. Among these acquaintances were
a number of young women who suddenly held a fascination for
Frederick—one in particular, whose identity remains a mystery.
Strong as this attachment might have been, several more years
would pass before Mears understood true love.

From time to time, he was invited to stay with his classmate,
Donald Stevens, in St. Paul. Frederick looked forward to those visits and especially to the daring and valiant stories Donald's father,
John F. Stevens, would tell them. This solidly built construction
engineer, with dark hair and a handsome mustache, was a highly
respected employee of J. J. Hill, founder and builder of the Great
Northern Railway. His true story of how he located the "Lost Marias
Pass" through the Rockies had won him renown in railroad history
and never failed to entrance the two boys.

According to Stevens' tale, at thirty-six years of age in the
spring of 1889, he had set out through the fog-ridden silence of
the forests to investigate a number of possible approaches to the
Rockies. With him were a saddle horse, a wagon, and a guide from
St. Paul. Growing impatient with the pace of the search, he sepa-
rated himself from the guide, put on snow shoes, and began plow-

Frederick, center, with friends and relatives at the family home.

ing his way through deep canyons of snow. Before realizing where he was, he had walked right into the Marias Pass. Then, to prove to himself that he had crossed the divide, he continued farther west before retracing his trail. Stevens' fortuitous discovery had shortened Hill's line to the coast by one hundred miles.

The story left a lasting impression on Mears. He admired the vigorous and straightforward manner of the man whose career in railroad construction had obviously been completely fulfilling. The more he learned about this kind of engineering, the more it instilled in him a desire to forge pathways through the wilderness himself.

Upon graduating with honors from Shattuck in 1897, young Frederick was certain of two things: he wanted to continue in his father's tradition by becoming a cavalry officer in the U.S. Army, and, just as earnestly, he wanted to have a part in the challenging crusade of building railroads into the western frontier. What he didn't know was how he could possibly achieve both. Battling enemies from the back of a horse was one thing; installing rail line for an iron horse was something else entirely.

**CHAPTER 2**

# SOLDIER AND ENGINEER

*It was just plain, everyday soldiering with the ever-*
*present chances of a bolo thrust from a seeming*
*"amigo" in the dark.*

Columnist Ashmun Brown
*New York Press*, 1914

In recommending thirty-six-year-old Mears for appointment
to the Alaska Engineering Commission in 1914, Colonel Goethals
was endorsing a man very much like himself at that age—dedicated
to army service, proficient in engineering, and confident in facing
the challenges of untamed territory. Having watched Mears in action for seven years, and having promoted him repeatedly to higher
levels of responsibility, Goethals knew he could trust the man to
turn out a first-rate job for the president.

Lieutenant Mears had already been working in Panama when Goethals arrived there in 1907 to assume the reins of command as chairman of the Isthmian Canal Commission and chief engineer for the project. Goethals had been appointed by President Roosevelt to fill the shoes of none other than John Stevens, once the Great Northern Railway's hero of Marias Pass and, more recently, the champion of the Panama Canal. Stevens' strenuous advocacy in favor of a lock system instead of a sea-level canal had won him wide acclaim.

Stevens himself had hand-picked Frederick Mears to serve on the Panama team. He did this for two reasons. First, he knew he needed men like Mears, as much for the man's dedication to a job as for his levelheaded skills in locating and constructing rail lines. Second, Stevens meant to make good on a longstanding promise he had made to Mears from his days with the Great Northern Railway.

## MASTER'S APPRENTICE

In 1897, when young Frederick graduated from Shattuck and took his first railroad job, John Stevens was his employer. Stevens had long sensed that Mears bore the markings of a railroad engineer, and his razor-sharp perception proved accurate. As Stevens himself had done, Mears would start at one of the lowest positions among laborers in a surveying gang and work his way up, solely on the merits of his performance.

The athletic young man's first assignment was in Minnesota, with the Great Northern's Fergus Falls division, as a survey party rodman. Carrying his rod into swamps up to his neck, over steep bluffs, and into brush-filled ravines, Mears took position wherever the instrument man directed him to go. Then, as a level man, he moved beyond mere mechanical labor and began giving directions to others. Before long, Stevens advanced him further to full engineer. In all, it took less than a year for Mears to demonstrate that he was entirely capable of taking charge of a survey party of his own although just twenty years old.

Meanwhile, J. J. Hill was adding branch lines from the main line of the Great Northern Railway in Idaho to the coal fields and gold mining regions of western Canada. Mears went next to British Columbia on one of these projects, with responsibility for planning and directing the engineering work. Then, when construction began, he was given full charge of one section and promoted to resident engineer.

Concurrent with this activity, the Spanish-American War was coming to a head thousands of miles away in Cuba. Dramatic newspaper accounts depicting courageous American men fighting and dying for the flag rekindled Mears' own patriotic instincts. He wanted to enlist but knew he was honor-bound to remain on the job until his assignment was finished. The choice must have been wrenching for him. Fit as he was and trained from childhood to be a soldier, he would have to wait another year before getting a chance to follow his father's lead.

By the time Mears completed his work in British Columbia, the Cuba campaign had come to a close. The U.S. had emerged victorious, and Cuba was born a debt-free republic. Spain ceded Puerto Rico and the entire Philippine archipelago to America. The Treaty of Paris was signed, and brass bands across the country trumpeted John Philip Sousa's new march, "The Stars and Stripes, Forever." While Americans celebrated, however, there was renewed unrest in the Philippines. Although the populace there welcomed its new state of independence, it was not ready to exchange one set of masters for another. President and generalissimo Don Emilio Aguinaldo was now leading a bloody revolt against the U.S., and American troops were dying in great numbers.

No longer bound by other commitments, Mears was ready to march to war. Turning in his final reports to Stevens, he asked for a leave of absence to serve in the Philippines. Stevens was probably not surprised by this turn of events. He must have known that, sooner or later, Frederick would join the army. Impressed by the young man's willingness to see his job through to completion, Stevens wished him well and assured him there would still be plenty of work for him with the railroads after the war.

*Mears collection*

Having enlisted in 1899 as an army private during the Philippine Insurrection, Mears advanced to the rank of second lieutenant of cavalry in 1901.

## JUNGLE WARFARE

In the autumn of 1899, Mears enlisted with the Regular Army, fully prepared to start at the bottom again—this time as a private—and work his way through the ranks. He was assigned to Company K of the Third Infantry, known as the Old Guard. His wages were $13 a month. On January 30, 1900, the 106 men in Company K joined several others in a battalion that left St. Paul by train for New York. The excitement and activity in that great city revived memories of Mears' youthful ambitions to board a steamer and sail to some unknown land. Now, the dream was about to come true.

A few days later, the entire complement of soldiers aboard the army transport *Sherman* sailed from New York harbor for Manila. The passage took almost two months, with stops at Gibralter, Port Said, Ceylon, and Singapore. It ended at Manila Bay, March 22.

Wearing light khaki uniforms, the battalion disembarked into the heat of the seaport city and marched directly to Lunetta Park, U.S. headquarters for arriving troops. Waiting for their orders, the soldiers could gaze westward to the blue rim of the bay, and see the outline of the island of Corregidor and the steep slopes of the Bataan mountains disappearing into the clouds. For a brief moment, it seemed they had come for rest and relaxation. But almost immediately, and for three years thereafter, they saw action.

Private Mears found the climate of the Philippines took some getting used to after the invigorating air of western Canada. As one observer remarked, "The heat of the country was the poison of the islands. There was no apparent air to breathe, only a gaseous substance which was more like a medium of warm soup."

In spite of the conditions, the brutal war continued without let-up. Private Mears and his fellow soldiers, scattered in small garrisons, hacked their way through the tangled jungles and snake-filled swamps to clear out the ladrones. Friendly Filipino scouts helped the troops locate and subdue the machete-wielding insurrectos.

Captives were liberated on the condition that they would take an oath of allegiance to the United States.

Mears experienced the bitter taste of war as he saw men beaten and boloed without mercy. But he fought hard and with the same enthusiasm that had won him success with the Great Northern. At various times during the war, he was stationed at Apalit, Bacolor, Santo Tomas and San Fernando. His dependable and quick response in battle was recognized by his commanding officers, who promoted him to corporal and then to sergeant.

Generalissimo Aguinaldo, meanwhile, had sought security in escape to the mountains. When he was finally captured on February 23, 1901, he reluctantly ordered his followers to lay down their arms. President Roosevelt, however, did not officially declare an end to the uprising until July of 1902.

Mears remained in the Philippines throughout that period. His superiors believed his ability as a civil engineer would be a great asset to him as an officer and promoted him to second lieutenant of cavalry. Thereafter, he was stationed at San Isidro and given topographic and construction responsibilities.

Before leaving the Philippines in 1903, Mears completed additional engineering assignments at the army officers school, located in Luzon. This qualified him to take the advanced course for officers at the U.S. Infantry and Cavalry School at Fort Leavenworth, Kansas. There, he would be assigned as an officer of the "hard-fighting" Fifth Cavalry, and would go on to encounter entirely new adventures that would change the course of his life.

As the transport *Sherman* passed the Hawaiian Islands on its return to California, Mears could reflect upon the beautiful land he was leaving behind, no longer at war. Images of the fighting and bloodshed were better forgotten but would always remain with him. At the same time, he had good reason to feel a deep sense of satisfaction and gratitude about the appointment he had just received to study at Fort Leavenworth.

Mears' mother and sister were waiting to greet him when he arrived in San Francisco. It had been three years since he'd seen them, and this visit was welcome, brief though it was. Any concerns he'd had for his mother's well-being were immediately allayed when he found her to be the very same self-assured woman she had always been. Elizabeth had acquired many new friends and had built a life of her own. Proud of her son's accomplishments as a soldier, she could be equally thankful that he now had the chance to succeed in his chosen field.

## FLYING COLORS

In the late fall of 1903, Lieutenant Mears and other student officers traveled together from San Francisco to Kansas. As the train rolled across the arid lands of Nevada, Mears could recall his father's stories about the rigorous winter he'd spent at remote Camp McGarry during General George Crook's campaign against the Paiutes. Bundled in clothes made of buffalo skins, the regiment had managed to survive there with only the most rudimentary of provisions.

Located near Kansas City on the west shore of the Missouri River, the post at Fort Leavenworth occupied several hundred acres of land. It had been built in 1827 by the historic Old Guard, the Third Infantry. Here the young lieutenant had his chance to practice wheeling and charging on horseback in field and terrain exercises, just as the soldiers he'd watched with envy as a child at Omaha Barracks.

He completed his courses at the infantry and cavalry school in less than a year and then enrolled for two more years of advanced study at the army's nearby Staff College. Through long hours bent over hefty engineering texts, he learned the use of precise instruments in the preparation of surveys and maps, and absorbed design processes for construction of basic truss, pontoon, and steel cable bridges.

Mears served as an aide-de-camp to Major General Franklin Bell, commandant of the service schools at Staff College, Fort Leavenworth.

Mears was considered by his instructors to be an exceptional engineer with a solid understanding of field fortifications and military law. He was equally considered by several members of the fair sex to be a perfect candidate for marriage. Few were aware that he had already proposed to the young woman from Ned's crowd in Portland. But, as time passed, he apparently began to question whether his feelings for her were real or imagined.

During his final years at Fort Leavenworth, Mears was appointed as an aide-de-camp to Major General Franklin Bell, commandant of the service schools at Staff College. For a short period, General Bell granted him a leave of absence to work as an engineer in the construction of a branch line for the Rock Island Railroad in Arkansas. While working there, Mears made occasional trips to Fort Clark, Texas, where he was able to continue friendships with some of the officers of the Fifth Cavalry.

## LOVE AT FIRST SIGHT

Fort Clark, with its expansive grounds of ancient oak and pecan trees, offered a pleasant retreat for the hard-working lieutenant. There, he could ride without a care across the surrounding miles of mesquite plains. On one of those visits, Mears met Jonathan M. Wainwright, also a second lieutenant of cavalry, who became a good friend. Tall and lanky, Wainwright had easily come by his nickname, "Skinny."

Like the senior Frederick Mears, Jonathan's father, Major Robert Page Wainwright, had grown up in New York City. He was descended from Peter Wainwright, the first Anglican bishop of New York. As a cavalry officer, he had lost his life fighting with Roosevelt's Rough Riders in the battle for San Juan Hill. Since the death of his father, Jonathan had been looking after the welfare of his mother and two sisters, Jennie and Helen. Mears was unaware at the time that Jonathan had begun to think of him as a perfect match for Jennie.

Mears astride his horse, Bird.

A year younger than Mears, Jennie was born at Fort Walla Walla, Washington, on St. Valentine's Day. As children, she and her brother gathered arrowheads while playing on the grounds at Fort Custer. Jennie was named for her grandmother, Jane Pound, and always considered her real name to be Jane, although she had been christened Jennie. At present, she was studying music and voice at the Chicago Conservatory of Music and planned an operatic career.

Mears had seen pictures of Jennie on his visits to Fort Clark. When they met, he could tell she was beautiful and intelligent, but

*Mears collection*

Jennie Wainwright at her most charming. Throughout her life she preferred to be called Jane.

there was something more. What was it that attracted him? The mystery may have been solved, if at some point he found himself thinking, "Dark hair, dark eyes, not as tall as mother but lively, and at the same time serious about life." Beyond that, she was the daughter of an army officer and an excellent equestrienne.

Mears took great pleasure in racing his horse, Bird, against Jennie's in a high gallop across the countryside. As their friendship grew, she accompanied him regularly to dances, concerts, and amateur theatricals held at Fort Leavenworth to break the monotony of garrison life. In no time, Mears had fallen hopelessly in love with Jennie, although he was still engaged to the Portland girl. Family memoirs reveal, "Everyone could see they were crazy about each other. It was like a storybook romance to the very end."

Late in 1905, in the midst of those lighthearted days, Mears received a letter from his mentor John Stevens, who by then was chief engineer of the Isthmian Canal Commission. Stevens had located the former cub engineer to whom he'd taken such a liking and was determined to get him to the Canal Zone. He guaranteed that he had more than enough for talented engineers to do. If Mears was interested, he would take steps to see that General Bell recommended him for service in Panama. Mears was pleased with the prospect of working again for Stevens and told him so in his reply. It took some effort on Stevens' part, but in 1906, true to his word, he managed to have Mears detailed from his regiment to proceed to the Canal and report directly to him upon arrival.

Surely thrilled with the chance to forge ahead in his career, Mears once again prepared to set sail to a different corner of the earth. As a soldier he had already circled the entire globe. En route to the Philippines, he'd had the singular experience of traveling through the Suez Canal and observing its operation. Completed in 1870, the waterway, in its day, was considered an amazing engineering achievement. Now, inspired by all of those vivid memories, Mears could let his imagination soar with visions of the role he might play in building a canal across the Isthmus of Panama.

PANAMA R. P.,                    DECEMBER 31, 1913

NEXT!

## CHAPTER 3

# CAMELOT IN PANAMA

*There are three diseases in Panama: yellow fever, malaria, and cold feet, but the greatest of these is cold feet!*

John F. Stevens,
Panama

Soft, billowing clouds. Verdant terrain. Boisterous birds. The idyllic sights and sounds were familiar as the ship came into port at Limon Bay, Panama. It was May 1906, and Frederick Mears was returning to the tropics. But this time, no enemy lay in waiting, save the uncompromising nature of the land.

Mears' traveling companions on the five-day voyage from New York included several other engineers and a large contingent of cranemen and steam-shovel operators. They all knew the task ahead would be monumental—cutting a waterway through the narrowest saddle of the mountainous isthmus joining the North and South American continents. But none of them could have imagined the full scope of the work until they encountered the scene face-to-face.

From the port, the group rode the small open coaches of the Panama Railroad to Colon, five miles distant. A welcoming party was there to greet them, led by John Stevens in person. Mears by now was a fair match to Stevens' powerful build and stood a few inches taller. The two shook hands heartily, glad to be working together again.

Stevens himself had come to Panama the year before as President Roosevelt's appointed chief engineer. The repeated resignations of several previous engineers had prompted Roosevelt to recruit Stevens on the recommendation of railroad magnate J. J. Hill. Having built bridges and tunnels and more than one thousand miles of railroad to date, Stevens was supremely qualified to take charge in Panama. On making the appointment, the president had warned him that things were in a "devil of a mess" down there.

## STEVENS PAVES THE WAY

Indeed, things in Panama were in disarray when Stevens arrived. Later he wrote, "I believe I faced about as discouraging a proposition as was ever presented to a construction engineer." The Isthmian Canal Commission appointed by Roosevelt (known as the ICC) had yet to meet to determine whether the canal should be built at sea level, and everyone on the construction site was waiting to be told what to do.

Before the U. S. took on the project, the French had already labored there for twenty years under the leadership of Ferdinand de Lesseps, builder of the Suez Canal. Blinded by the success of that project, he refused to acknowledge the differences between the level, rainless sands of Egypt and the rocky hills and flooded

Collection of CZBrats

John F. Stevens, the Hero of Marias Pass.

jungles of the Isthmus. The fact that the French had been unable to rid the area of yellow fever and malaria had also contributed to their failure.

Some claimed the French undertaking was simply ahead of its time, but American efforts had floundered as well, even with new developments in construction technology. Divided responsibilities and bureaucratic delays were partly to blame for the lack of progress. Of greater significance, however, was the fact that huge numbers of workers were fleeing the Zone in fear of contracting yellow fever and malaria, which had already killed hundreds of others.

When Stevens arrived in July 1905, he saw at once that no useful work was going to be accomplished until the problem of disease was solved. The men had to have clean, habitable living conditions before they could be expected to endure long hours of hard physical labor and remain committed to the project. Stevens wasted no time in taking control of the situation. He lent full logistical support to army physician Colonel William Gorgas, the ICC's sanitary engineer, in his ongoing efforts to cleanse the area of mosquitos. Panama City and Colon were fumigated many times over. Exhaustive measures were taken to purify the water supplies, and thousands of men were employed to tear down expendable structures and build anew. By the end of the year, Gorgas and Stevens had succeeded in eradicating yellow fever and malaria from the Zone.

From the beginning, Stevens easily gained the support of the workers. He was out on the line daily, whatever the weather, smoking a black cigar and going about his work in rubber boots, overalls, and a battered felt hat. "Big Smoke" Stevens, as he was called, considered the construction of the canal to be basically a railroad undertaking. He recruited only railroad men for the job and employed the biggest, heaviest equipment possible. He also recognized, as the French had not, that the existing Panama Railroad could serve as the lifeline for the project, smoothly and efficiently moving men and materials to and from the work. As a result, the concept of construction railroads was taken to a new level.

Now, welcoming Mears and the other new recruits, Stevens began explaining how he planned to upgrade and expand the trackage of the old Panama Railroad to accommodate a system of work trains. These would function within the enormous ditch as a vast conveyor belt, rolling continuously beside the steam shovels digging out several levels of earth at once. Never before had so many work trains been used in such a confined area. Stevens' resourcefulness in adapting the power of railroad equipment to the task at hand set a valuable example for Mears.

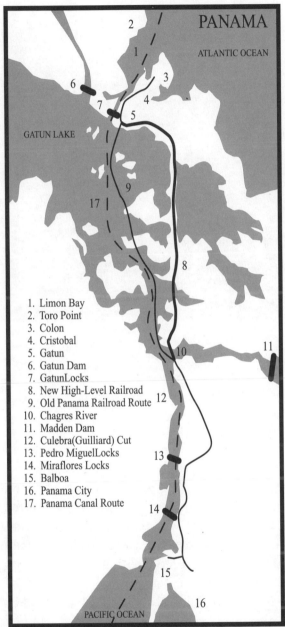

1. Limon Bay
2. Toro Point
3. Colon
4. Cristobal
5. Gatun
6. Gatun Dam
7. GatunLocks
8. New High-Level Railroad
9. Old Panama Railroad Route
10. Chagres River
11. Madden Dam
12. Culebra(Guilliard) Cut
13. Pedro MiguelLocks
14. Miraflores Locks
15. Balboa
16. Panama City
17. Panama Canal Route

The Panama Canal Zone, showing the route of the old Panama Railroad (9) and the relocated section built under Mears' supervision(8). The dotted line indicates the ship route through the canal.

The Culebra Cut, Panama in 1911.

The next day, the men re-boarded the train waiting to carry them to the small native village of Gatun seven miles away on the banks of the mighty Chagres River. From there, they journeyed on to Culebra Cut, the site of the principal excavation. Once called the "Grande Tranchee" by the French and currently referred to by the Americans as simply "the Cut," this man-made canyon was about nine miles long. Only upon seeing it and the maze of railroad tracks laid out on its floor, could the men fully grasp the magnitude of Stevens' endeavor.

Mears soon learned that his first assignment would be as track foreman in the canal excavation. Once on the job, he and other engineers would direct the installation of the standard-gauge track to accommodate the heavy machinery that would excavate and haul away thousands of cubic yards of earth from the Cut. When completed years hence, the Cut would plunge 350 feet, nearly to sea level, and extend to a width of 300 feet at its deepest point. By one estimate, a work train of cars loaded with the total excavation at Panama would be long enough to circle the globe four times at the equator.

## A CHANGE OF COURSE

One pivotal decision remained. The ICC was still debating whether to build the canal at sea level or with locks. Originally, Stevens had thought his plan for the removal of millions of yards of earth and rock would produce a sea level canal, and the ICC had supported that concept. But during the rainy season, when the flooded Chagres River triggered endless landslides, obliterating months of work, Stevens knew he could no longer endorse that procedure. Instead, he favored an alternative approach that had been considered earlier, namely to dam the Chagres River, thereby inundating more than 160 square miles of land, and creating an artificial lake. A system of locks at both ends of the lake would make up the differences in sea level.

Within weeks of Mears' arrival, Stevens was called back to the capital to defend his position before congressional committees. He did everything in his power to persuade legislators that creating a lake and building a canal with locks was the only solution. Finally, on June 29, 1906, Congress approved his plan.

After returning to the Isthmus, Stevens recognized that thirty-two miles of the old Panama Railroad, running parallel to the survey line for the canal between Gatun and Pedro Miguel, was in the way of the work and would have to be moved. His plan was to build a new high-level railroad that would follow the eastern border of the proposed Gatun Lake. In September, Stevens appointed Mears assistant engineer for that relocation project under Ralph Budd, a distinguished civil engineer who was in charge of construction.

*Mears collection*

Mears, fourth from right, led survey parties into the swamps of Panama in preparation for relocating portions of the Panama Raiload.

In connection with this work, Mears' assignment was to make a field survey for the new rail line through the tangled wetlands of the Isthmus. A cadre of knowledgeable, toughened inhabitants of the area accompanied him on that forage, along with his surveyors and engineers. They set off in long, dugout canoes piled high with survey equipment, camping gear, and rifles. With monkeys chattering in the trees overhead, pumas prowling in the shadows, and crocodiles lurking in the mangrove swamps, the men had to be constantly wary as they inched their way into the jungle overgrowth. Much of that vegetation had to be cleared before actual construction of the new railroad could begin.

Part of the new line was to cross Gatun Lake on high embankments. Because decaying vegetal matter lay between bedrock and the surface, the earth sank under the weight of the rock fill brought in from the Cut to build the roadbed. Repeated loads of material had to be added to broaden the base and to reinforce the embankments before they could support the heavy railroad equipment at the required height.

*Mears collection*

Building the high-level railroad along the eastern shore of Gatun Lake.

By the time the job was finished, the railroad relocation portion of the Canal project, by itself, would consume close to $9 million and a full five years of labor. Upon seeing the new rail line in operation, John Barrett, director of the Pan-American Union remarked,

> The whole roadway, though limited in
> mileage, is operated with the skill of a great
> system. It is remarkable how smoothly it is run
> without mixups, collisions or accidents when
> it is interlocked everywhere with all the side
> and switch tracks used by the canal dump trains.
> Its rolling stock compares favorably with the
> best roads of the United States.

None would dispute that Stevens' achievements in Panama were remarkable. His work had received the unqualified endorsement of the president. His construction railroads would remain

*Collection of CZBrats*
Colonel George W. Goethls, successor to John Stevens in Panama.

the fundamental operating procedure in the Cut until the excavation was finished. Even so, in February 1907, he abruptly tendered his resignation, emphasizing that finishing the project required the expertise of a hydraulics engineer and that he had very little experience in that area.

Stunned and annoyed, Roosevelt concluded that only a military man could be counted on not to quit, because duty to his country would demand that he complete the job. Thus it happened that George Washington Goethals, a colonel in the Army Corps of Engineers, was chosen to replace John Stevens. At forty-nine, Goethals had accumulated an impressive list of accomplishments in his career. The lock he designed and built for the Muscle Shoals Canal on the Tennessee River had drawn particular acclaim. A West Point graduate, he believed that army officers ought to have a practical knowledge of railroading as a preparation for modern war. To his mind, the 40-mile Panama Railroad, when finished, would be well worth the cost for its military value alone.

Colonel Goethals officially took over as both chairman and chief engineer of the Isthmian Canal Commission at the end of March 1907. As such, he would have total decision-making authority—something Stevens had never enjoyed. And he would remain to finish the work Roosevelt had enlisted him to do.

## JANE BRIGHTENS THE SCENE

Jennie Wainwright, now Jane, was puzzled and hurt that Frederick had left for Panama without making any definite commitment to her. He longed to write her a proposal of marriage, but he was not free to take that step until he could bring amicable closure to his attachment to the girl in Portland. When he finally proposed, Jane accepted in an instant.

Mears sent frequent letters describing the life they would be sharing. Sometimes he enclosed newspaper clippings about the work, once including a full account of President Roosevelt's tour of the Zone. It became his custom to send photographs and postcards to his family and friends from wherever he happened to be, always adding a humorous remark to let them know he was in good spirits. One photo of himself smiling broadly under a Panama hat and sporting a stiffly starched suit carried the caption, "When Reuben Comes to Town." In another photo of slain crocodiles stretched out on a flat-bed rail car he wrote, "Crocs out for a joy ride."

Early in March 1907, upon receiving notice of his promotion to first lieutenant, Eleventh Cavalry, Mears submitted a request for personal leave to be married. In less than three weeks, he was on his way. While waiting in Costa Rica for his departure orders, he sent Jane a picture postcard of workers from Barbados, Martinique and Jamaica displaying huge limbs of bananas. This time he wrote, "Have a banana, Johanna. See you in a few days. Fred." His nickname for her became "Johnnie" and remained so throughout their marriage.

The wedding took place on April 6, in the post chapel at Fort Clark. The couple's happiness radiates from photographs taken on that day, as they posed flanked by groomsmen in full cavalry regalia and bridesmaids in long white gowns. Mears' leave was short, however, and the two soon left by train for New York. From there, they took a steamer to Panama.

The newlyweds arrived in Limon at the height of the season when all of the foliage was its most luxuriant. En route by train to Colon, Jane marveled at the beauty of the tropical landscape and the giant cedro trees arching overhead. The voyage to the Canal Zone, and the first few months of getting settled, amounted to an extended honeymoon for Frederick and Jane. All of the waiting and uncertainty were now things of the past.

They lived in the small town of Cristobal, not far from Colon, in one of the large two-story frame houses remaining from the French period. From a wide, screened-in veranda that surrounded the upper floor they looked out on a cluster of tall palm and ceiba trees. Brightly colored birds of every hue imaginable

*Courtesy Marilyn M. Richards*

Frederick and Jane Mears were married April 6, 1907, at Fort Clark, Texas. Jane's brother, Johnathan M. Wainwright, stands second from right.

The Mears home in Cristobal, Panama.

regularly visited the bamboo and orchid plants below. The interior of the structure had been modeled to accommodate two engineers and their families. When Mears discovered the mahogany walls of their place had been painted a medicinal white for sanitary purposes, he enlisted some local help, scraped all of it off, and refinished the wood.

With the arrival of their baby daughters, Josephine (Jo) in 1908 and Elizabeth (Betty) in 1910, the Mearses' quarters were enlarged accordingly, as was the distaff part of their household. The place was filled with nursemaids, cooks, laundresses, and grandmothers who took turns visiting. Little Betty never forgot how their Jamaican nurse would put a large crab on the floor and start it crawling toward her when she dawdled about getting dressed. Other times Betty and Jo, with pennies in their hands, would wait patiently on the front steps of their house to buy a treat from the mango woman who often stopped by with a large basket of fruit perched on top of her head.

Although Mears' work load was demanding, the young couple thoroughly enjoyed their years in Panama. On their one day off in the week, they picnicked with friends on the beach at Toro Point across the bay from Colon or joined hundreds of other employees for sightseeing excursions by rail to Culebra Cut. The largest social occasions of the year were the Saturday night dances at the Tivoli Hotel, where the ICC's 26-piece band played their favorite tunes, "Way Down in Jungle Town," "Moonlight Bay," and "Alexander's Ragtime Band."

*Mears collection*

Mears with daughter Betty in Panama.

GOETHALS TAKES CHARGE

Intensely absorbed in all aspects of his work, Colonel Goethals
directed activity with a brusque, authoritarian style. Because his education and training had come entirely at public expense, he firmly
believed he owed it to the public to stay until the canal was finished.
He expected his employees to be loyal to that goal above all else.
While they may not have liked his autocratic manner, his willingness to hear grievances personally from any worker, regardless of
rank, won him their solid admiration.

By early summer, 1907, Goethals had begun harnessing the
waters of the wild Chagres River to create Gatun Lake where lush
vegetation and several small villages had once stood. The resulting
Gatun Dam would rise one hundred feet in height and extend 1.5
miles in length. His scheme for controlling water entering the canal
from both the Atlantic and Pacific oceans involved twelve enormous lock chambers with 700-ton steel gates between them. Made
of gleaming white concrete, each chamber measured one thousand
feet long, 110 feet wide, and six stories high. More than 4.5 million
cubic yards of concrete were poured to build them. A single one of
the chambers, if stood on end, would be taller than the Eiffel Tower.
In short, the concept was colossal; few could truly fathom its scope.

In 1909, the resignation of Ralph Budd as chief engineer of
the Panama Railroad Company prompted Goethals to promote
Mears to the vacancy. The final phases of the railroad relocation
work called for Mears to design and build a bridge span over Gatun
River and a reinforced concrete pier for the railroad terminal at
Cristobal. In response to a directive from Washington, Goethals
also enlisted him to take charge of the location survey for a 350-
mile rail line between the Canal Zone and the Costa Rican boundary. When the army sent an inquiry as to Lieutenant Mears' availability for service elsewhere, Goethals shot back directly that he
could not be spared.

Before long, Mears found himself responsible for constructing the New Washington Hotel at Cristobal. Coincident with its

completion, a delegation from Washington came to examine operations in Panama. While the visitors enjoyed their stay in the luxurious, pseudo-Moorish hotel, they questioned Roosevelt's highhanded launching of the government into the hostelry business without congressional authority. One legislator declared, "I don't believe it's legal. I strongly suspect the whole business is unconstitutional."

"That," responded Goethals, "is not a matter of concern to me. I got an order from my commander-in-chief to build this hotel, and I built it."

On another occasion, a team from Capitol Hill visited the Canal Zone to investigate mounting costs. Some members of the group complained that employees were being paid too much and that their quarters were too comfortable. When one of the more outspoken congressmen insisted on inspecting the upstairs of Goethals' own home, the colonel physically barred him. The angry lawmaker demanded to know whether, on his own salary of $7,500 a year, he would be given a place like the ones he had just seen, if he were to work on the Isthmus. Goethals cooly replied, "Sir, if you worked in the Canal Zone, I don't think you would make $7,500 a year."

Encounters such as these made an indelible impression upon Mears, who would be called upon to respond to similar inquiries at the height of his own career. His completion of the high-level railroad was a success story in itself. By May 1911, trains were making regular two-hour runs between Colon and Panama City for commercial purposes as well as for construction hauls. In an average month it carried some 50,000 tons of Pacific coast products on their way to the eastern seaboard. Mears predicted confidently that the canal would be open for traffic in time for San Francisco's Panama-Pacific International Exhibition scheduled for August 1914. "We have had remarkably little trouble with labor," he told newsmen. "There are no clouds on the horizon in the Canal Zone."

Mears' time estimate proved accurate, in spite of the clouds that came. All work on the canal was forced abruptly to a stop on

January 19, 1913, when the most voluminous, persistent, and famous of the slides, known as Cucaracha, snarled the railroad tracks, blocked traffic, and wiped out months of work. On Goethals' thought-for-a-day pad was printed, "Life is just one damn thing after another." One of his aides couldn't help but notice that the colonel had marked out the word, "thing" and substituted "slide." The only remedy was to dig it out again.

Later that year, Goethals promoted Mears to general superintendent of the Panama Railroad and of the company's steamship line, in addition to his responsibilities as chief engineer. This placed him in charge of a fleet of six large ocean-going vessels plying the waters between the Canal Zone and New York. Few admirals then had as much tonnage under their command as had the young lieutenant.

In this capacity, Mears regularly hosted visitors connected with his work, and the couple's social life soon extended far beyond the earlier Saturday night dances. Betty's recollections of her parents dressed for dinner in those years remained vivid. To her, the two of them seemed like exalted creatures, her mother in sparkling evening gowns and her father in white linen suits. Still, in the midst of the glamorous and cosmopolitan life he was enjoying, Mears missed the punch and mental stimulation of being actively engaged in engineering projects. He was always more comfortable working outside than dressed to the hilt for social obligations. In fact, as far as he was concerned, the time was ripe for change.

## A SUMMONS TO WASHINGTON

William Howard Taft had succeeded Roosevelt as president in 1909 but lost his bid for re-election to Woodrow Wilson in 1913. By then, Congress was considering another major construction effort beyond the immediate boundaries of the United—this time to build a railroad across the raw territory of Alaska. It would be the first time the U.S. government had undertaken railroad building to such extent, and this enterprise would be enormous. When news was released of the government's plans for Alaska, with a budget of $35 million, understandably Mears began to contemplate how the project—equal in size and complexity to the Panama Canal—could be just as challenging.

Wilson strongly favored the idea of opening up the northern domain of the U.S. He saw the railroad as the most expedient way to reach the coal and other resources held there. In his State of the Union address in December 1913, he had declared that one key to Alaska's storehouse would be a system of railways open to all. "We must use the resources of this country," he said, "not lock them up." One of his first actions as president was to establish a commission to oversee the railroad construction, following the model of the ICC in Panama.

It was during this period that Colonel Goethals was called to Washington to advise Wilson and Secretary Lane about possible candidates for the president's commission. His excursion there was surprisingly brief. He saw in no time who would be best for the job and in his no-nonsense style set the gears in motion for Mears' appointment. In fact, the young man was within weeks of being chosen to oversee construction of the railroad in Alaska.

As he began to envision the northern work, Mears may have welcomed the opportunity to escape the tropical heat. Grateful for Goethals' confidence in him, the lieutenant resolved to continue to probe the field of engineering with the same zeal the colonel and Stevens had displayed in building the Panama Canal. Another door had opened, and Lieutenant Mears was proud to march through it.

One last trip on "his" Panama Railroad gave Mears a chance to reflect upon all that he and his men had accomplished. At the same time, he remembered how the construction traumas of the canal had seemed to vanish when everyone witnessed the opening of the sea gates for the first trial of the locks in September 1913. The moment lasted less than two minutes, and the lock system operated smoothly thereafter. By August 1914, the Panama Canal would be ready for use.

After news of Mears' appointment was made known, the *Panama Herald* reported that he would sail for New York on April 22, 1914, on the *Calamares*. The newspaper commended him as a capable engineer and praised him for the fine relationships he had established with his employees. Many were begging him to remain.

Likewise, when Jane and the girls left fourteen days later, a news writer observed that in the life of the Zone Jane would be remembered for her solid common sense and for those qualities which would make any man proud and happy to be her life's companion. "The lieutenant may conquer Alaska without her," said the reporter, "but with her it will be a sure thing."

CHAPTER 4

# THE LURE OF ALASKA

*I do not object to having my department raided for men of ability, but would like to know of it in advance.*

Secretary of War
Lindley M. Garrison, 1914

Entrusted with the task of building a railroad of monumental proportions across Alaska, Mears applied himself to learning as much as possible about the territory before he left Panama. Then, on board the *Calamares* en route to the U.S., he had more time to study the literature and books he'd gathered and to review the packet of information Lane had sent him regarding the new work. William Healy Dall's observations about upper Cook Inlet particularly caught his interest because the commission would be investigating that part of Alaska in conjunction with its preliminary surveys. The renowned geologist had noted that the area contained heavy concentrations of coal and had tremendous potential for agricultural development.

Dall's glowing portrayals of Alaska also explained the lure the territory held for settlers and miners. Back in the late 1800s and early 1900s, prospectors wanting to reach the interior took steamers from Seattle to the Russian trading post at St. Michael, near the mouth of the Yukon River. From there they traveled by riverboat up the Yukon into the mining areas around Fairbanks and on into the Klondike. Other hardy souls approached by land over hazardous routes into Dawson, Yukon Territory, to reach the golden treasure. Years later, though, long after the gold rushes, the wilds of the northern domain were still without any real road: in summer, travel was by boat or pack train, and in winter, by dog sled. From this, Mears could understand why development of the territory had not advanced more rapidly.

## GOVERNMENT OR GUGGENHEIM

Even without proper roads, budding entrepreneurs in Alaska had managed to ship quantities of timber, fish, coal, and copper to markets in the States. Predicting the rapid depletion of Alaska's resources, powerful conservationists under the leadership of Gifford Pinchot warned that future generations would have nothing upon which to subsist unless those resources were protected. At the same time, the Guggenheims' Alaska Syndicate, which had long monopolized trade in the territory, was beginning to feel threatened by the competition. They joined the conservationists in urging President Roosevelt and Congress to enact legislation that would prevent "wanton exploitation of the land and its resources."

In response to their persistent lobbying, Roosevelt issued an executive order, withdrawing coal lands from "location and entry" and other lands previously discovered in Alaska that contained valuable resources. Those withdrawals, together with the legislation already in place governing homesteading in Alaska, created a hardship on those who were actually working the land. Small railroaders, without tonnage and coal to fire their engines, were forced to give up.

An example of the frustration felt by those early pioneers came forcibly to the attention of the nation in May of 1911, when an Associated Press article, "The Cordova Coal Party," appeared in leading newspapers across the country. It described how intolerable the situation had become for the people of Cordova who, in sheer despair, had emulated the Boston Tea Party by throwing a cargo of imported British Columbia coal overboard. Their own valuable coal deposits, within reach, could not be mined because of the restrictive land withdrawals. That incident alerted the nation to their plight, and soon the cry, "Open Alaska!" echoed across the land.

Congress clearly had a problem. It was unwilling to provide financial guarantees or exclusive privileges to private railroad pioneers, and yet there was something obviously wrong in a situation where a territory twice the size of Texas had no rail service.

Roosevelt's successor, William Howard Taft, made the first real effort to address the situation. He asked that a commission be formed to study and recommend rail routes in Alaska for developing the country and its resources. Congress, though, began to balk at underwriting a venture of such far-reaching proportions. Some lawmakers feared that government ownership of the project would usher in an era of socialism. The strongest opposition came from enterprising railroaders already in Alaska who wanted to control rail transportation in the territory. But finally, in August 1912, Congress signed into law an act directing President Taft to form a commission to proceed with his plan.

By the time Woodrow Wilson assumed the presidency, the Taft commission had completed that assignment. Their recommendations languished, however, while debate on the pros and cons of the subject continued as before. When factious interests threatened to stall the project altogether and possibly lose it for the territory, Alaska's lone delegate, James J. Wickersham—who had authored and introduced the original Alaska railroad bill—saved the day on January 14, 1914, in a five-hour speech before Congress. At the conclusion of his eloquent address, Wickersham asked, "Who will control Alaska? Will Congress serve as a trustee for the little people or will the Syndicate control?" After stating emphatically, "The choice is Government or Guggenheim," he received a thunderous ovation.

All of these events made it plain to Mears why Wilson was disinclined to rely on the Taft report alone in making his decision about where to locate the railroad in Alaska. Instead, the president sought comparative data and had elected to send a new team of engineers to the territory to collect it. The undertaking could still become bogged down in bureaucracy, though, even with the blessing of Congress. Mears needed only to reflect on Stevens' fight for locks in Panama to comprehend what might lie ahead.

## WILSON'S NEW TEAM

It was at the end of April 1914, when the president's appointees met one another in person. Mears was introduced first to William C. Edes in the offices of Secretary Lane. A senior railroad engineer, Edes was a lean, weathered gentleman who for forty years had been locating and building railroads through some of the most difficult stretches in the mountains of the west for the Southern Pacific and Santa Fe lines. To Mears he seemed a friendly, fatherly sort of person. Born in Boston in 1856, Edes had graduated from the Massachusetts Institute of Technology in 1875. At the time of his appointment to the president's Alaska commission, he was chief engineer of the Northwestern Pacific Railroad in California.

*Mears collection*

The Alaska Engineering Commission, appointed in 1914 by President Woodrow Wilson: William C. Edes, seated, Thomas Riggs, left, and Frederick Mears, right.

Thomas Riggs, forty-one, joined the Alaska team a few days later, and Mears took an immediate liking to him. The lively man, born in Ilchester, Maryland, had studied at Princeton University from 1890 to 1893. He was well known in Alaska and the Yukon as a mining engineer and as chief surveyor on the International Boundary Commission. Riggs was definitely not one of Delegate Wickersham's political choices for the AEC because, prior to his selection, he had been endorsed by many for governor of Alaska. The fact that Wickersham had gubernatorial aspirations of his own no doubt dampened his enthusiasm for Riggs.

For several months Mears had anticipated meeting President Wilson. On greeting Mears, the trim, gray-haired man in the familiar pince-nez glasses was surprisingly aloof. Wilson's handshake seemed weak, but those who knew him well simply accepted that as part of his nature. After a time, Mears came to understand that the strength of Wilson's leadership lay in his profound knowledge, his unquestioning faith in democracy, and his unbounded self-confidence.

In contrast to Wilson, Lane was a Napoleonic looking man with a firm handshake that matched his personality. A Canadian by birth, but raised in California, he was possessed of a restless ambition which had led him to careers in journalism, law, and inevitably politics. After unsuccessful bids for governor of California and mayor of San Francisco, Lane had come to Washington when Theodore Roosevelt appointed him to the Interstate Commerce Commission. His policy as Secretary of the Interior was conservation by use. In confidence to his family Lane once wrote, "A wilderness, no matter how impressive or beautiful, does not satisfy this soul of mine. It is a challenge to man. It says, 'Master me! Put me to use! Make me more than I am!'"

Unbeknownst to the new commissioners, Lane was preoccupied with ambitions for Alaska which went far beyond railroad building. He wanted the appointees to relieve him of the construction and management details of the project, thereby enabling him to seriously engage in his other plans for broader development in

Alaska. Once, Lane admitted privately that he would like to spend a few years of his life just dreaming about what could be done up there. He believed the "huge territory" ought to be able to support thousands of Americans.

The approximately forty interlocking bureaus controlling development in the territory were of constant concern to Lane. Their problems were chronic. With little or no understanding of Alaska, each bureau was jealous of the others' authority, and all were ill-disposed to work in harmony. At one point, Lane had suggested the formation of an advisory board in Alaska to guide and expedite its development. He advocated controlled growth of the territory over the unprincipled use of the land. Eventually, though, Lane would realize he must give his full support to the railroad project alone.

A month before the three commissioners first met, Congress had appropriated $1 million to carry out the commission's initial activities, to be used until expended. In the interest of good stewardship, it had also directed the president to acquire, by purchase or condemnation, existing privately owned railroad property within the territory and to ship to Alaska all excess rail equipment and property from the construction of the Panama Canal.

Some critics of the project believed that those who advocated construction of the transportation corridor had neglected to consider that a railroad must carry tonnage in order to make it pay. From the inception of the project, however, it had never been intended that the railroad would be a profit-making venture. Those who understood the situation were in agreement that years would pass before its income would exceed its indebtedness.

## A HASTY SOLUTION TO A THORNY PROBLEM

In conjunction with the commission's first meetings, Mears was called upon to travel to New York City to consult with the engineers who had prepared the 1913 Taft report. Prior to leaving Washington, he stopped for a visit with the Secretary of War, Lindley M. Garrison. Surprised to learn that Mears was headed for Alaska, the secretary asked who had authorized his service there. Mears named Secretary Lane as the authority, adding that he had received his appointment from the president, through an act of Congress. Garrison was disconcerted by the news but politely continued in cordial conversation with the young lieutenant. Mears then bid his colleague good-bye and went on his way to New York, completely unaware of the trouble that was about to brew over his appointment.

Secretary Garrison immediately began examining the law again, even though he had read it dozens of times before. It gave the president authority to designate only civilian engineers and officers of the engineer corps of the army. Wilson was within his rights when he appointed Edes on Lane's request, but he had no authority at all to name Mears because army appointments were restricted to the engineer corps. Lieutenant Mears was a cavalry officer.

For its part, the Army Corps of Engineers took as a serious affront the fact that Colonel Goethals—one of their own—had recommended a cavalry officer for the work. Their complaints soon reached Lane. He, however, was so thoroughly impressed with Mears' performance in Panama, and with Goethals' recommendation, that he decided to have the appointment validated over the objection of the Corps of Engineers. With the stroke of a pen, Lane drafted a joint resolution that quickly sailed through Congress to settle the matter. This special act of Congress, which authorized the president to appoint Lieutenant Frederick Mears, by name, for service on the commission, passed on May 13, 1914.

When Mears returned to the capital, he was shocked to realize how close he had come to missing his opportunity to work in Alaska. No doubt, the fact that he needed to be detailed at once before any work could begin, had enabled the weary legislators to come to a quick acceptance of his appointment. But it was because Lane had persisted that Mears kept his job.

Rejoining one another in the AEC offices within the Department of Interior, the three appointees conferred again with Lane. It was their consensus that the new commissioners would immediately travel to Alaska to direct and oversee preliminary surveys of all possible rail routes. In the fall, they would consolidate their findings and prepare a report for the president. Before concluding their meeting, they designated Edes, the eldest, to be chairman of the commission. Mears, the most robust and energetic of the three, would then be free to explore the expanse of the territory they were to cover: from the vicinity of Portage Bay, on Alaska's southcentral coast, to the headwaters of the interior.

It saddened Mears to leave his family to close up what had been their enormously happy home for eight years in Panama, but there was no turning back. He was beholden to the army and was expected to leave at once. Now, with such names as Corozal, Cucaracha, Las Cruces, and Cristobal still echoing in his ears, he would soon be called upon to familiarize himself with Susitna, Matanuska, Kuskokwim, Tanana, and other place names of Native American or Russian origin. Mears was impatient to see with his own eyes the land of endless summer days and equally long winter nights—the land that once had been called William H. Seward's "Ice Box."

*Get Mears!*

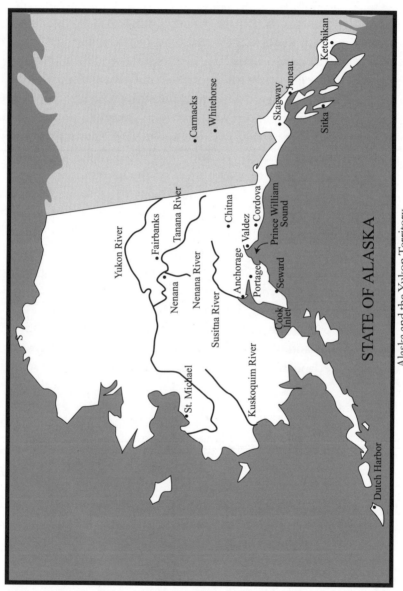

Alaska and the Yukon Territory

**CHAPTER 5**

# PRELIMINARY SURVEYS, AFOOT AND AFLOAT

*The outstanding genius of it all was the man who found the way. . . .*

President Warren G. Harding
Nenana, Alaska, 1923

Early in May 1914, Chairman Edes, Lieutenant Mears, and a small clerical staff proceeded from Washington D. C. to Seattle by train. Thomas Riggs would travel later. At every stop along the way, the men were besieged with reporters clamoring to know where the rail line would be located. Each time, they politely explained the essential terms of the Alaska railway bill, emphasizing that the final decision would be made by President Wilson.

Reluctant to stake their reputations solely on findings from the earlier report by Taft's appointees, the commissioners were relieved to have free rein to conduct the preliminary surveys in Alaska. Now, with Wilson's backing, they would be able to broaden the scope of their work unhampered by the 1913 investigation.

In his eagerness for the swift development of Alaska's resources, Lane was urging the commissioners to locate the railroad near the coal fields and close to the most direct water connections. That in mind, and with conclusive evidence about the quality and quantity of coal in the Cook Inlet region, they continued with their plans to set up a headquarters camp in the wilderness area of Ship Creek, at the upper end of the inlet. In order to thoroughly cover the areas in question, they selected two additional bases of operation: one at Seward (the former headquarters of the old Alaska Northern Railroad) and the other near Fairbanks in the interior.

On arrival in Seattle, Edes and Mears set up an office in the Alaska Building. From there they organized the purchase of supplies and materials to be shipped to Alaska, including 125 horses. They had planned to recruit surveyors primarily in Alaska, but they accepted applicants from San Francisco and the east coast as well, in order to avoid any appearance of favoritism. Eleven surveying parties, each under the direction of a skilled engineer, were to search possible routes to the interior. In addition, the Seward contingent was to examine alternative routes along the Kenai Peninsula, including a topographical survey of Passage Canal.

## CELEBRITIES OVERNIGHT

Seeing that their city stood to gain as a major distribution center, Seattle businessmen wanted to establish friendly alliances with the new commissioners. As a result, the three engineers were invited to more functions than they were able to attend. At a luncheon given them by the executive committee of the Alaska

Bureau and trustees of the Seattle Chamber of Commerce, they were asked about Alaska and exactly where the railroad would be located. Their preliminary reviews on paper led them to favor a western route beginning at Seward, but they were in no position to reveal their preferences now. Edes' clever response provided the needed levity.

"I cannot tell you much about Alaska," he said. "I have never been there, and I am afraid if I started to tell you what I do know, I would be apt to get into what I do not know and that would take a very long time."

Because of the distance involved, Riggs and his party set out for Alaska ahead of the rest. They were to evaluate the property and condition of the old Tanana Valley Railroad in Fairbanks. Their circuitous journey took them by steamer to Skagway, by rail to Whitehorse, then overland 150 miles around the still frozen lakes to Carmacks, where the party took a river steamer to Nenana. From there, Riggs' survey crews would head south into the Alaska Range, following the banks of the Nenana and the Jack rivers, until they reached Broad Pass. If all went as planned, they would there tie in with a preliminary line brought north to the same point by other crews from Ship Creek.

An advance party of workers, hired to build the construction camp at Ship Creek, left Seattle May 26, 1914, on the steamer *Dirigo*. Eleven days later, their vessel reached the waters of upper Cook Inlet. It dropped anchor near the small town of Knik, because docking facilities at the creek were limited at best. In the late 1800s, Knik had been a thriving supply center for trappers, gold seekers, and mining districts in the north. Now, skippers of scows and launches from the little town were standing by, ready to transport the laborers, materials, horses, and supplies from the *Dirigo* to the shores of Ship Creek.

Mears and Edes, meanwhile, finished organizing their work in Seattle. When they left for the territory, a large contingent of engineers accompanied them. All were *cheechakos*, a term they'd soon learn means newcomers to Alaska.

## CONTENDERS FOR THE TERMINAL

En route to Juneau, the territorial capital of Alaska, the men were taken in by the spectacular beauty of the land. As their steamship slowly maneuvered its way through southeastern Alaska's Inside Passage, they saw mile after mile of snow-capped mountains, glaciers, and heavily forested landscape. In the distance, whales thrust their black forms into the air and blew steam like water-bound locomotives. Gulls, murrelets, and hundreds of sea birds skimmed along the surface of the water, and schools of porpoise raced through the ship's wake. Never, in the rugged country of the northwest nor in the tropics, had Mears' emotions risen to such heights as they did when he approached the vibrant land. The only regret was that Jane could not be with him to share the excitement of the moment.

Entering Gastineau Channel, the party could view the imposing Alaska-Juneau Gold Mine. A small, narrow-gauge dinkey locomotive standing in front of the mine was one of hundreds used in early mining endeavors in Alaska. A short distance from the mine, the compact city of Juneau clung precipitously along the base of Mount Juneau.

A throng of residents and city officials standing on the wharf gave the railroad engineers a rousing welcome as the ship pulled into port. Then Edes and Mears took a tour of the capital. With charts and graphs rolled under their arms, they visited one government office after another, describing the work they hoped to accomplish in Alaska. The comprehensive nature of their plans, the size of the group, and the caliber of men soon to be descending upon Alaska were proof enough for doubters that this time the government meant business: a railroad through the heartland of Alaska would become a reality.

The commissioners' next stop was Skagway, gateway to the Klondike, to investigate the narrow-gauge White Pass & Yukon Railroad, built after the 1897-98 discovery of gold in the Yukon. This was the first railroad to scale Alaska's alpine rampart and reach the interior. The engineers had never intended to suggest the use of this line as a staging area for the government railroad because it ran through Canadian territory, and lacked a broad resource base. However, their inspection of the line did provide graphic insight into the immensity of the task that lay before them.

Cordova and Seward were rival claimants for the privilege of serving as the southern terminus of the railroad. Near Cordova, the engineering team observed first the damage that the Baird and Childs glaciers had inflicted upon the bridges and roadbed of the Copper River and Northwestern Railroad. Then they encountered the enormous rotary plow that had been used during the winter to remove heavy buildups of snow caused by prevailing winds from the Copper River Delta. On seeing this, the engineers concluded that, although a workable railroad existed, future traffic would require a major overhaul of the entire line.

Townspeople crowded around the commissioners when they stepped off the ship at Seward. Residents were pleased because their town was under consideration as the first link in the rail line that would connect the tidewaters of the Pacific with the interior of Alaska. It was immediately obvious to the engineers that the promoters of Seward's Alaska Northern Railroad believed their town would be chosen not only as the terminal but also as the headquarters for the entire project. Far from convinced, the commissioners tactfully withheld any comment. They had yet to investigate an expansive land mass situated closer to the Matanuska coal fields and mineral resources of the interior.

The engineers were astounded by the condition of the once proud Alaska Northern Railroad. It clearly was in worse shape than the facilities of the Copper River and Northwestern Railroad. They estimated that to render a safe operation of only light trains along the railroad's seventy miles of track would require an immediate expenditure of $500,000 and ultimately close to $1 million over a period of years.

Another possibility remained: the Passage Canal-Portage Bay route. This narrow strip of land on the Kenai Peninsula lies between Prince William Sound and Turnagain Arm, an estuary of

Cook Inlet. The Taft report had not considered it, but Mears, the army man, saw its potential. His calculations had always been directed to the best—not necessarily the easiest—solution. He recognized that the route could provide a closer alternative link to the interior and another access corridor altogether in the event of a war.

In its report, the AEC later would state that it found no obstacles to prohibit the development of port, townsite or terminal facilities within that area. "A track through the Kenai Peninsula's neck is possible, if the railroad is bored beneath mountains, 13,005 feet through the eastern mass and 4,960 feet through the western section." It is a credit to the AEC's 1914 survey that the line installed in that location decades later, from Whittier to Portage, covered almost exactly the same ground.

After comparing their observations with government data and information from master mariners, the engineers concluded that railroad terminal facilities could be built at any of the harbors considered suitable. They reasoned further that, to optimally develop Alaska's resources, the railroad system would not be dependent upon selection of any particular harbor. This conclusion irritated the Seward promoters, who felt their harbor was far superior to all others under consideration.

Riggs and his surveyors working in the interior, meanwhile, studied old rail routes that could be upgraded to connect with the coal fields and mining operations in the area. One possibility was the Tanana Valley Railroad, a 44-mile narrow-gauge line that ran from Chena, at the head of steamboat navigation on the Tanana River, to the mining town of Chatanika, about fifty miles north of Fairbanks. Upon close investigation, Riggs found the railroad's equipment to be in poor repair. In his short summary of existing railroads elsewhere in the northern region he wrote, "On the Seward Peninsula two little rail-lines slumber peacefully on the Arctic tundra. A few other short stretches of construction in various parts of the territory serve strictly local demands or are out of commission entirely."

## THE VISION TAKES SHAPE

As chief engineer, Mears was to determine a possible route to Fairbanks through the Alaska Range. Information from a survey performed by the Alaska Central in the winter of 1905-06 had confirmed the Broad Pass route as a feasible location for a railroad. This pass forms the watershed between the Cook Inlet drainage on the south and that of the Tanana River on the north. Mears intended to inspect the route himself in the summertime to verify the absence of any obstacles to railroad construction in the area. He further wanted to check the progress of survey parties already in the field.

When he was sure the crews working in Passage Canal and along Turnagain Arm were in control of their assignments, he took the first opportunity to proceed to Ship Creek and points beyond. Motoring into Cook Inlet aboard a gasoline launch, Mears and a small staff marveled at the magnitude of the mountains that were their constant companions on the way. Two hundred miles north, standing in perfect clarity, were three of the highest peaks on the North American continent: McKinley, Foraker, and Hunter.

History was made in this region in 1778, when English explorer Captain James Cook, with his vessels the *Resolution* and the *Discovery*, entered these waters looking for the long-sought-after Northwest Passage. Over time since then, Russian trading posts, Alaska Native settlements, and prospectors' camps had occupied the area. Now Mears, plying the broad waterway and reviewing his charts, saw the expansive government land he had envisioned while back in Washington. As he drew closer, two high plateaus came into view. Covered with tall stands of spruce and birch, they stood prominently on either side of Ship Creek draining into the inlet. When the men landed, the air resounded with the cries of hundreds of white gulls circling overhead and crowding the moss-covered banks of the creek. A king salmon run was underway, and they were ready for it.

Tall, sturdy, and self-assured at thirty-six, Mears was a commanding figure as he strode ashore. Stepping onto the wooden planks across the gray glacial mud near the water's edge, he saw the workers had things well in hand. They had constructed a barn and corrals for the horses and had erected tents for their own use. Now they were busy framing in the commission's field offices.

Earlier in the summer, when the first crews landed at Ship Creek, they had noted six people living in the vicinity. Jack Brown and his wife, Nellie, occupied a log cabin near the mouth of the creek. A forester for the Chugach National Forest Service, Brown had come there in 1912. Another forester, Keith McCullough, lived nearby, and the J. D. Whitneys had a homestead four miles up Ship Creek. At the foot of what is now known as Government Hill, a small cabin housed a squatter by the name of Thomas Jeter. With the arrival of the AEC, Ship Creek was beginning to take on the appearance of an orderly camp. While the commission remained uncertain as to where the president would choose to locate the rail line, crews were moving ahead to prepare the site for all of the workers who would be returning in the spring.

In late June, Mears began his reconnaissance of the route to Broad Pass. Accompanied by an assistant, he set out on horseback to follow the eastern wall of the Susitna Valley. The men traveled just above timberline in order to observe the country to be traversed by the survey. From the top of Bald Mountain they had a broad, un-hampered view of the land below. Looking due south down Knik Arm and Cook Inlet, they saw the plain stretching out from the foot-hills toward tidewater and the town of Knik. Dotted with small lakes and ponds, this lowland lay covered with dense stands of spruce, cottonwood, and birch. Continuing due north, the men found that any railroad could seek its location on practically a free grade, so little did the general elevation of the country change.

The men left high ground on July 1, and proceeded toward the confluence of the Susitna and Chulitna rivers. Just beyond that point, they saw that the terrain on the western bank of the Susitna would be more favorable for travel with pack animals. Up to this time, they had crossed streams by fording or swimming, but the Susitna, now in flood stage, was far too wide and swift to cross in that manner. Not willing to take that risk, Mears and his assistant rolled up their sleeves and set about building a raft from dry cottonwood. Once completed, the craft was large enough to transport the men, their supplies, and their three horses to the opposite bank in one trip.

Continuing north along the west side of the river, they traversed flat land until reaching a narrow canyon. Ascending into the hills, they followed the course of the river to Indian Creek. This led them into Chulitna Pass, and from there, they continued on through Broad Pass. Mears encountered three of his field crews at points along the way and finally met up with Riggs at Moody Creek. Riggs had made his reconnaissance from Fairbanks across the Tanana Flats to the Healy coal district. The two parties proceeded together down the Nenana River to the Tanana. From there, a river steamer took them to Fairbanks.

All this while, another reconnaissance was underway farther to the west. J. L. McPherson and his crew were surveying another possible railroad location from the vicinity now called Willow through Rainy Pass to the Kuskokwim River and on into the Iditarod gold district. Though besieged with rain and bad weather, they covered a phenomenal 726 miles on foot by September. Completing their work just in time, they caught the last boat down to the Yukon River delta before freeze-up.

Mears emerged from his reconnaissance experience fully confident that the AEC had succeeded in locating a route for the railroad through the Alaska Range. Now he knew it was indeed possible to connect the tidewaters of the Pacific with the headwaters of the interior. He detailed a small crew to winter over at Ship Creek to maintain the AEC's field headquarters there, serve as weather observers, and take care of the stock and equipment. Later in September, with their mission accomplished, the commissioners and surveyors sailed for Seattle where they were welcomed by associates and masses of laborers seeking employment. Everyone wanted to hear what had happened up north. It was clear that those who had returned were now confirmed boosters for Alaska as the "Land of Promise."

Back in their Washington offices for the next several months, Edes, Riggs, and Mears consolidated their field notes, charts, maps, and profiles of the land. In addition, they prepared cost estimates of the work ahead and evaluations for the possible purchase of the Tanana Valley Railroad and the Alaska Northern Railroad out of Seward. On February 11, 1915, the three engineers signed their report and transmitted it to Wilson. In it, they offered no specific recommendation for the location of the railroad. Their mission had been to collect the evidence and present it in as impartial a form as possible. The final decision would be up to the president.

This map of the railroad route through the mountains appeared in a local paper around 1920.

CHAPTER 6

# ALL ABOARD
# FOR THE LAND OF PROMISE

*Dump him down in the wilderness before the coming of steel, and he ipso facto becomes the "government."*

Columnist Jack Lincke,
*Anchorage Daily Times*, 1921

Suspense mounted as the time approached for President Wilson's selection of the route for the railroad in Alaska. During the waiting period, speculation regarding the government's $35 million investment in the territory was running high, and Secretary of the Interior Franklin Lane became a very popular person. Each new day, his anteroom filled with another group of politicians, real estate investors, bankers, and railroad entrepreneurs desirous of having a role in the expenditure of those funds. Some of them wanted Lane to urge the president to consider the purchase of their railroads for the main rail link to the interior. Their hopes and dreams would hang in the balance until Wilson made his decision.

In essence, Wilson's options boiled down to choosing between an eastern or a western route, or endorsing them both as Taft's advisors had recommended. The eastern route would begin at the port of Cordova, follow the Copper River & Northwestern rail line to Chitna, and continue north to Fairbanks. The western (Susitna) route would begin at Seward, incorporate the Alaska Northern line to Turnagain Arm, proceed past the Matanuska coal field, and then on to Fairbanks. The first option would be shorter but showed less promise for agricultural development; the second required more rail miles but would pass through richer land. Either one would guarantee the "all-American" line that supporters championed, but each posed major logistical problems. The cost of taking on both at once would be prohibitive.

## HEAVYWEIGHT RIVALS

Of those who frequented Lane's crowded waiting room two distinguished looking gentlemen, Senator Simon Guggenheim and J. P. Morgan, dressed in black business suits and stovepipe hats, overshadowed all of the others. They were the managing partners of the Alaska Syndicate, which owned and operated the Copper River and Northwestern Railroad to serve their rich Kennicott copper mines. They were also the owners of a dozen Alaska salmon canneries and the Alaska Steamship Company, which carried their ore and fish to markets in the States. They had long held a monopoly over the political and economic activities of Alaska.

John Ballaine, founder of Seward, Alaska.

A rival from Alaska waiting to see Lane for similar reasons was John E. Ballaine, a natty, energetic railroad owner, nearly bald, with a carefully clipped mustache. Never allowing himself to be overlooked in the scheme of things, this man would become one of Mears' major adversaries. His history reads like a saga of what went wrong. He had dreamed of making a fortune in Alaska, but very few entrepreneurs who came to the territory during the turn of the century realized instant wealth—with the exception of prospectors who struck gold. His vision of building an all-American railroad from the tidewaters of the Pacific to the interior of Alaska had never reached fruition, and yet it was an idea whose time had come.

Shortly after 1900, following an earlier geographical survey of the area, Ballaine had explored possible rail routes to the interior. As a result of those investigations, he had become convinced Alaska needed a railroad. As a young Seattle realtor and newspaperman, and a veteran of the Spanish-American War, he scraped together $2,000 in soldiers' script and $4,000 in cash, with the help of his brother, Frank. This made it possible for him to acquire the Lowell homestead on the Kenai Peninsula, property which later became the nucleus of the town of Seward. Not wanting to risk losing his initiative, the doughty man moved quickly. He invited a large group of Seattle businessmen to consider, as he had, the return on investment if the railroad were built. They agreed to support him, and in March 1902, with capital of over $30 million, they organized the Alaska Central Railroad Company.

Before long, in an effort to maintain the momentum of the venture, Ballaine formed the Tanana Construction Company and took out a contract from the newly formed Alaska Central Railroad to build the railway to the interior. By 1904, a terminal, wharf, and dock had been installed at Seward. But one year later, the railroad company had exhausted its funds, having completed only twenty miles of the roadbed. Unfortunately, the investors had not considered the added costs of building in the north.

This was a great disappointment to Ballaine. But, not willing to give up, he organized a herculean fund-raising campaign across the country to arouse the interest of other friends, capitalists, and associates in completing the project. Two financiers, A.C. Frost of Chicago and H. C. Osborne of Toronto, jumped at the chance to build a railroad in Alaska. They made an offer Ballaine could not refuse, starting their negotiations at $2.5 million. Soon after, backed by the Sovereign Bank of Canada to the extent of $3.5 million, with a contingent promise of up to $18 million more, they took over the line. The Shedd Syndicate of Chicago and all others who had previously invested in the project were paid off. Frost and Osborne bound themselves individually with Ballaine to complete the Alaska Central. Frost became president, and Ballaine continued to hold a minority share of the stock.

The new investors built the road to mile 47. However, in 1908, the bankrupt project was forced into receivership. Although the Sovereign Bank of Canada rescued the project and renamed the line the Alaska Northern Railroad, construction again closed down when funds gave out after completion of only twenty-five more miles. The track ended at Kern Creek, mile 72, at the head of Turnagain Arm.

By then, Ballaine was almost at his wit's end. In a last-ditch stand to save the Alaska Central-Alaska Northern Railroad, he traveled to New York where he approached the Morgan-Guggenheims. He proposed that they refinance the Alaska Central as a narrow-gauge line under his direction, but they turned him down. Although their Copper River and Northwestern Railway had not crossed the Alaska Range into the Tanana Valley, they were adamant that if any railroad should breach the mountains it would be theirs alone. Rebuffed, Ballaine never forgot the high-handed treatment he had received from them.

Discouraged but not defeated, Ballaine turned his attention to Congress and asked the government to take on the project. In 1914, when the enabling act was passed directing President Wilson to establish a commission to build and construct the railroad, Ballaine's foot was in the door. He was not about to take a back seat during the deliberations. And, when it became clear that the government was going to undertake the enterprise, Ballaine was sure lawmakers would reward his efforts by purchasing the ailing Alaska Northern Railroad and his speculative property at Seward.

Ballaine and all the others waiting to learn whether the president was interested in their proposals were sorely disheartened when Lane informed them the president had no intention of giving preferential treatment to anyone. Wilson planned to base his decisions regarding the project solely upon the information his engineers had given him. This was not what Ballaine wanted to hear, but he withheld his reaction until Wilson's choice was made public.

In April 1915, the cherry blossoms were in full bloom in the capital when the president finally relayed his decision to Secretary Lane. Emerging from the White House with the official news, Lane was astonished to see the mass of people crowded on the portico and milling about on the green lawn of the mansion. Some had been waiting several hours to hear what he would say. Regaining his composure, Lane informed everyone that the president had selected the Seward-Fairbanks route. This would open up territory that had not been served before and would connect with two of Alaska's great coal fields, one at Matanuska and the other near Nenana and the Tanana River.

In anticipation of Wilson's decision, the number of those applying for employment with the railroad had risen to 10,000. Consequently, Lane took advantage of the moment to warn those expecting to find immediate work in Alaska that they would be largely disappointed because the first few places were to be awarded on the basis of merit and experience. Then, before closing his remarks, Lane announced that he had been directed to initiate the purchase of the Alaska Northern Railroad.

On hearing the news, Ballaine found victory at last: his property holdings in Seward would increase in value, and the Alaska Northern would be redeemed. Even so, he questioned the AEC's hiring policies and directed those who published his newspaper, the *Seward Gateway*, to inform readers that Lane's announcement

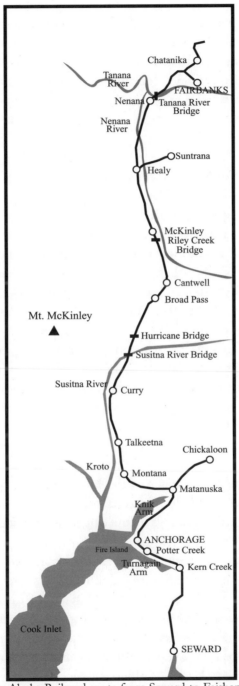

The Alaska Railroad route from Seward to Fairbanks.

implied that he intended to keep the poor people out of Alaska. In time, Mears and the other commissioners would discover that the Seward newspaper often resorted to conjecture when it released news about their activities. Ballaine was on his way to becoming the self-appointed watchdog of the AEC.


## MARSHALING MEN AND MATERIALS

Lane went along with the commission's plan to follow the same distribution of work it had established during the preliminary survey. Edes at Seward was to direct the reconstruction and operation of the Alaska Northern. Riggs' division was to survey the final location of the most northerly segment of the line out of Fairbanks, which would join Mears' central section at Broad Pass.

Mears was responsible for four major projects to be initiated almost simultaneously: constructing a terminal on the flat land of Ship Creek; installing new rail south from there to connect with the end of the old Alaska Northern line near Kern Creek; building the main line north to the Matanuska River with a 38-mile branch line to the neighboring coal fields; and continuing toward Broad Pass with another 160 miles of track beyond the junction at Matanuska.

Mears was no stranger to the hiring process, having already proven himself capable of recruiting hundreds of workers in Panama and carrying out all of the exigencies implied in an undertaking of such magnitude. Respected by his friends and associates, he had many contacts from former railroad work who were of great help to him. Among them were Ralph Budd, his early supervisor in Panama and now chief engineer and president of the Great Northern, and of course, John Stevens, with whom he remained in touch. In conjunction with this activity, Mears made trips to interview with Canadian railroad engineers in Winnipeg and Vancouver. He hired at least one of the Alaska Northern's former employees as a result.

Thomas Riggs, left, directed the AEC's work south from Fairbanks to Broad Pass, while Mears and his crews worked north to Broad Pass from Ship Creek.

Apart from finding capable workers, the lieutenant's primary concern at the moment involved the lack of adequate docking facilities at Ship Creek. Until he had something in place there, he would be at the mercy of shippers who were devising all sorts of schemes to derive excessive profits from handling the commission's freight. Not wanting the project to be held hostage by opportunists, Mears resolved to build a wharf of his own.

While in Seattle, he assembled everything he needed to build a floating dock. He purchased a 1,000-ton barge from a towboat company and arranged with them to have it delivered to Alaska. Then, after three smaller scows and a knocked down 200-ton scow were loaded on the barge, his dock was ready for shipment. Next, he purchased a complete pile-driving outfit with a 15-ton stiff-leg derrick, operated by a hoisting engine, to lift the cargo and hired an experienced pile-driving crew to sail with him to Alaska aboard the *Mariposa*. He planned to use that equipment to build a gridiron with a pile foundation to furnish level bases upon which the fleet of scows would rest during the changing of the tide. He was acutely aware, however, that until the channel was dredged, deep-draft steamers could not dock at the port.

*Mears collection*

Mears devised a temporary floating dock at Ship Creek, 1915.

When Mears left Seattle on April 19, 1915, every berth and inch of steerage on the vessel was occupied. He wrote to Jane that upwards of 500 flag-waving people had come to watch and cheer when the ship departed. Some of the well-wishers related that not since the rush to Dawson or Nome had there been such a sight at the port. Once in Alaska waters, he found every coastal town along the Inside Passage equally enthusiastic in greeting the arriving ship.

The celebrations in Seward were endless, following Lane's announcement that their town was to be the southern terminus for the government road. One evening's event at the Moose Hall saw a joyous crowd singing "Tipperary," Tom McConaty, the "wingfooted Scotsman," tripping the light fantastic, and a boxing match featuring George Kosmos, the "greased lightning" Greek.

But, even in the midst of the merrymaking, there was an air of doubt. Many questioned whether the decision regarding the location of the route was firm. Others brought up statements they had read or heard that a railroad system to best develop the resources of Alaska was not dependent upon the selection of any particular harbor or current population center. Still, to reinforce their best hopes, the city fathers constructed a 35x5-foot lighted sign to greet the *Mariposa* at their port. It read, "Seward, The Terminal."

## FIRST THINGS FIRST

As soon as the ship was secured to the dock at Seward, reporters rushed over to ask Mears when work on the railroad would begin. Knowing how impatient they were, but hesitant to reveal the extent of the work planned farther north, he replied, "Not a word will I say—absolutely, not a word, flat footed!" The following day, the *Seward Gateway*'s banner headline declared, "Mears Silent as a Sphinx."

The commissioners were firm about discouraging stampeders from coming to Alaska. They did so because, as railroad historian William Wilson observed, "They wanted to avoid a 'hell on wheels' situation and hoped to provide for a smooth transition from wilderness to town." But news about the railroad traveled fast, even in those days. Despite the warnings, when Mears arrived at Ship Creek, he was overwhelmed by what he saw: a rambling array of white tents and shacks erected on the very land where he intended to build the construction camp.

Every boat entering the harbor had brought more and more tradesmen and persons seeking work, until almost overnight a tent town with a population of two thousand souls had come into being. Masses of railroad construction workers joined hundreds of other pioneers who had come to Alaska not because of the popular lure of gold but to put down roots in a land that offered them hope and a promise for the future. Water sold for five cents a bucket, a wagon and team rented for two dollars an hour, and sanitation, if it existed at all, was rudimentary.

Still, Mears was heartened to see how much his crews had accomplished in his absence. He admired the log structures they had built from on-site stands of spruce and noted the land-office business the gas-powered boats from the small town of Knik were enjoying. Their services were in big demand for transporting new arrivals, orders of foodstuffs, and rough green spruce between Knik and Ship Creek.

*Mears collection*

Businesses of all kinds aimed to meet the needs of Tent Town inhabitants.


On reaching the outpost, Mears had intended to begin immediately the important work of connecting Ship Creek with the Matanuska coal fields. But a quick survey of the chaotic tent town gave him pause. Looking into the eager faces of the many who clamored to greet him, he changed his mind. His first responsibility, without a doubt, would have to be for the welfare of those settlers. In this one instant, he established a relationship with the townspeople that gained him their enduring respect.

*Mears collection*

Artist Sydney Laurence took this panorama of Tent Town in the summer of 1915.

The nagging question running through his mind at that time was how to carry out the orderly transition he wanted. To keep the men occupied, he put as many as he could to work handling the supplies and construction equipment that were lightered to shore with the arrival of each incoming steamer. Day laborers were paid $3 per eight-hour day, and other classes of more skilled labor a higher rate. Realizing he needed a suitable place to care for injured men, Mears acquired a partially completed log structure and started carpenters to work putting it in shape to be used as a field hospital.

Soon the time approached to ask the settlers to move off the terminal lands. In order to avoid a minor uprising, Mears posted notices around Tent Town informing everyone that the new town-site on the plateau south of Ship Creek would soon be available. Then, he tactfully asked the settlers to begin making preparations to move their dwellings. At the same time, he assured them he had

*Mears collection*

Workers laid track across the mud flats to the water's edge so that cargo could be hauled from incoming barges to higher ground.

Arriving shipments were loaded onto carts and transported across the mud flats at Ship Creek.

no desire to cause any unnecessary inconvenience but explained that the commission would need all of the ground currently occupied by the tent camp.

Mears had great respect for the people who came to the wilderness with the intention of starting the town. With no regulation or organization, little disorder had erupted among them. A long delay in making the land available, however, could cause problems. As the population grew, people became noticeably restless. To avert any outbreak of trouble, Mears asked Edes to obtain Lane's support in prohibiting the issuance of liquor licenses at Ship Creek. He was convinced, if saloons were permitted to operate, turmoil and frequent arrests would certainly follow. The living environment needed to be safe, especially for the sake of women and children.

*Mears collection*

Ship Creek with the *Standard* in the foreground, 1915.

## THE DISTAFF ARRIVE

Jane Mears and her daughters came to Ship Creek early in May. Jo, now seven, and Betty, now five, were brimming with excitement to see their father and their new home. Like many on board the vessel, they had become seasick crossing the rough and stormy Gulf of Alaska. But, when they caught sight of great pods of whales breaching in the distance, they forgot about being ill. Now, as the vessel approached Ship Creek, the long journey was about to end. They were thrilled at the sight of the Chugach Mountains emerging from their mantle of snow. The place was a beehive of activity. The staccato of pile drivers crashing and carpenters hammering reverberated everywhere.

Anticipating more work than she alone could manage in settling her family in the frontier town, and expecting another child late in the year, Jane had brought with her two Jamaican women to help with the girls and the chores—one a governess and the other a maid. Both wore dark uniforms with white aprons. On the surface, they appeared to be well prepared for the tasks ahead. But, the moment they saw the primitive living conditions, they refused to disembark and chose instead to return to the States on the same vessel that had brought them north.

A scow carried the sisters and their mother from the ship to shore, where workers helped them out of the boat onto the heavy planks that led up to the construction camp. Wanting her girls to look pretty for their father, Jane had dressed them in the blue velvet coats with ermine collars that they had worn while living in the capital. Stepping gingerly over the slippery wooden walkway, Betty broke into a gleeful run the moment she saw her father and promptly fell flat on her face in the mud. This, she related years later, was her first "impression" of Tent Town.

The only solid building in Tent Town at the time of the family's arrival was the log hospital. The cottage intended for them, on the hill above the terminal yards, had yet to be finished. While they waited for its completion, the Mearses joined in with the other settlers, occupying a plank-floor tent of their own, cooking over a wood stove, and burning kerosene lamps for light. Recalling that

*Mears collection*

The AEC hospital under construction in foreground.

summer, Betty claimed it was the best camping experience they
ever had.

As long as the makeshift community remained on the terminal lands, however, serious construction of the railroad's line to the
Matanuska coal fields could not begin. Mears wanted to proceed
with that vital work but was in no position to ask the people to
move until Lane issued the new townsite regulations.

Cramped in their quarters and distressed by fears of contagion and water contamination, the settlers became increasingly critical of the government's inaction. They demanded to know why the
new townsite was not ready. Mears, feeling the pressure, wrote urgent letters to Lane pleading for no more delays. But Lane was too
far removed from the situation to comprehend its urgency. Had the
workers, unshaven and caked with mud, appeared in his anteroom
to plead their case, he might have paid closer attention.

**CHAPTER 7**

# TRANSITION FROM
# WILDERNESS TO TOWN

*Anchorage is our child, and we are responsible for
its well-being until it can care for itself.*

William C. Edes,
AEC Chairman, 1915

Without regulations for the new townsite, Mears was equally
as frustrated as the settlers. He had no authority to let anyone occupy the land, and until the people removed their dwellings from
the railroad construction yard, his own work was on hold. But,
knowing how quickly Lane had succeeded in gaining congressional
support to have him transferred for work in Alaska, he was certain
the secretary would find a way to move the project forward.

AEC office buiding at Ship Creek.

And so it happened that, just in time, Secretary Lane sent instructions to Clay Tallman, administrator of the General Land Office, to proceed with the survey for the new townsite. Less than three weeks later, Tallman's appointee, Andrew Christensen, arrived at Ship Creek with a surveying party. As a young lawyer, Christensen had worked closely with railroad traffic administrators in the northwest. In 1910, he had traveled to the territory to mediate coal land cases for the federal land office. He and Mears, about the same age, knew one another from earlier meetings in Washington. Both were native sons of Nebraska.

As the two men were not strangers, they immediately went to work making on-the-spot decisions. Even so, the survey and preparation of the townsite was a time-consuming task. After the clearing and grubbing of the heavily forested area, the denuded land smoldered with stumps, logs, and muskeg. No one could walk on it without burning his boots. This was a discouraging situation for the would-be settlers, who could see the land they hoped to occupy, smoking on the plateau above their encampment, but could not get to it. To allay their concerns, Mears posted more notices about the Tent Town assuring everyone that the government's survey of the land was almost complete and that, as soon as the townsite regulations were official, the area would be opened for their inspection.

Such was the state of affairs at Ship Creek on June 19, 1915, when the townsite directives were finally placed in Mears' hands. They gave the commission the go-ahead to reserve lands for public purposes and to survey other potential railroad townsites along the rail route. In addition, they included rules for the appraisal and sale of lots and provided for the appointment of a superintendent to direct an auction of the land. Mears knew he could rely on Christensen to conduct the auction, having observed his competency during the townsite survey. He wrote Lane to that effect, adding that the land officer's knowledge of the area would serve him well when he appraised the property. Lane concurred.

Before the regulations were established, Mears had asked Lane to include a provision that would impose stiff penalties and forfeiture of property and payments if any lots were sold or used for the purpose of manufacturing, selling, or disposing of intoxicating liquor, or for gambling, prostitution, or any unlawful purpose. Mears was not an abstentious individual; he enjoyed his snifter as regularly as the next man. Nevertheless, when the regulations arrived with a proviso abolishing the sale of liquor, he was grateful that Lane had understood the seriousness of the situation.

## ON THE AUCTION BLOCK

As the time for the land sale drew near, Mears, anxious to proceed with construction in the terminal and beyond, was more than ready for the auction to take place. He asked Christensen to urge the settlers to vacate all of the land in the encampment directly after the close of the sale. Christensen shared Mears' concern and adapted his prepared speech accordingly. The event was held in Tent Town at Ship Creek on July 10, 1915.

The sun beat down on the assembled throng that day and upon the bald pate of the auctioneer. Even though it was the height of summer in Alaska, many of the men wore dark business suits and felt hats for the occasion. Christensen, somewhat formally dressed as well, stood behind a lectern on the reviewing stand. A large chart nearby depicted the 350-acre townsite. Everyone appeared eager for the sale to begin. First, Christensen thanked his talkative listeners for helping the AEC maintain an orderly camp at Ship Creek. Then, with very little fanfare, he urged them to move their dwellings to the new townsite immediately after the completion of the auction.

"From personal observation," he parlayed, "I have seen some of you businessmen come in here, erect your tents and do business before the departure of the boat which brought you. Now if you

The townsite auction, July 1915.

can do that in that case, there is no reason why you cannot also do it when you move."

He then briefly outlined the country through which the rail- road would pass and praised the resources tributary to it. "Many have asked," he said, "What does this mean to us? Will this place be only a temporary construction camp during the building of the railroad?" Ship Creek, he quickly assured everyone, by all means would continue to be the construction base for building the spur line to the Matanuska coal fields, plus the line north to Fairbanks, and would serve as a major shipping point.

In reemphasizing the permanency of the town, he indicated on the chart where a large tract of U.S. government land, called the Terminal Reserve, had been set aside for expansion of the railroad. Lands along the shore in that reserve, offering fine views of Cook Inlet, also were assigned for future development of a wharf. Before closing his speech, Christensen informed everyone that the townsite regulations had also designated reserve lands for municipal use, for federal buildings, for a school, a cemetery, parks, and for Indian possessions.

Railroad construction workers had come to the auction because it offered them a once-in-a-lifetime opportunity to purchase a piece of reasonably priced property. Others attracted to the sale had traveled from all parts of Alaska and from the States hoping to be proud owners of land on the last frontier. Encouraged by Christensen's speech, those standing about the auction platform were spirited in the bidding on every lot offered for sale, especially business property. L.G. Nyberg of Seattle offered $825 to beat out all other bids for a choice piece of commercial land originally appraised at $400. The highest bid of $1,150 came from G. M. Campbell. In describing the event, the *Cook Inlet Pioneer* claimed, "Anchorage broke all previous records in two hours' time when 600 lots were sold for $148,000." Some lots went for a minimum of $75. Not one person succeeded in getting a lot without competition.


THE TOWN SETS ANCHOR

After the auction, an immediate mass exodus of settlers began from the flats of Ship Creek. Teams of horses pulled the temporary canvas and frame dwellings uphill to the higher ground of the new townsite. Once there, buyers scrambled to find the lots they had just purchased.

The town plan followed a stock, grid pattern commonly used by other railroad towns in the western states and territories. North-south streets were named alphabetically, and east-west streets were numbered. The main thoroughfare, known today as Fourth Avenue, looked like a setting for a wild west movie. Eighty feet wide, it was lined on both sides for more than a mile with tents, frame buildings, and wooden sidewalks. Beyond the main street, hundreds of small houses and tents with wood floors had been erected here

B78-75-3 *Anchorage Museum of History and Art*
Horsepower moved Tent Town off the flats up to the new Anchorage townsite.

and there. Only stumps of trees gave evidence that the area once had been densely forested.

Many of the stores and shops in the new town were rudimentary structures at best. A one-story shed served as a clothing store where trousers, coats, and long rubber waders hung by nails from the walls. A white canvas sign in front of the establishment was so large that it covered half of the building. A mattress factory consisted of a tent with a stovepipe running high above the canvas. Dust and smoke blew over the merchandise stacked outside. A large "queen's ware" store had crockery and porcelain of all sorts displayed at the entrance. Some structures served both as houses and as storefronts.

Advertisements bordering the front pages of each edition of the *Cook Inlet Pioneer* attested to the permanency of the town and promoted many opportunities for diversion that were available to the hard-working residents. In addition to announced events and

AEC Cottage No. 6, where the Mears family lived from 1915-1916.

informal gatherings, proprietors of the Inlet Soda Company sold quantities of mineral water, soda, cider and syrups that summer. A variety of motion pictures billed by a small theater became a popular pastime. Captain Jack Hadland, master of the commodious power boat *Red Fish*, offered $1.50 round-trip fares twice daily from Ship Creek via Goose Bay to Knik. For those needing or wanting to travel, the Admiral Line steamers published regular departure schedules. Most of the residents' time that first year, however, was taken up with the details of establishing their homes and businesses.

In the flurry of activity, Mears and his own family were caught in the throes of moving, too. By this time, Jane's camping experience had begun to wear thin, though not for the children, who hoped it would never end. Their house, AEC cottage No. 6, on the bluff directly above the construction terminal was one of fifteen similar structures built by the commission in a birch and cottonwood grove, reminiscent of a quaint summer resort. Expecting a third child in December, Jane and her husband were more than ready to inhabit four solid walls.

## JETER'S EVICTION

Some inhabitants of Tent Town took their time moving out of the terminal grounds. One of them was Thomas Jeter, who had settled there in 1912. His cabin and barn stood on lands of the terminal reserve when the first contingent of railroad workers had arrived. Jeter was proving to be a troublesome character. He had rejected all efforts to reach a settlement, even after learning his buildings would jeopardize the commission's plans to put several hundred men to work constructing a storage warehouse. Jeter stood firm. He had no intention of moving, and he engaged the services of his cousin, a former lieutenant governor of California, to assist in his defense.

According to his testimony, Jeter had tried to acquire the land he occupied as a homestead, although it had not been listed, platted or eliminated from the forest reserve. Had he accepted the offer of a forest service officer to identify his plot by metes and bounds, his tract could have been listed with the Secretary of Interior. The sum of his efforts, it appeared, was no more than an attempt to obtain land which the federal government was not ready to sell.

Faced with a possible lawsuit, Mears sought the assistance of Edes and Lane in Washington. As a last resort, Lane directed Mears to confer with Assistant U.S. Attorney William A. Munley stationed in the new townsite, and to take whatever action he considered appropriate. Recognizing the seriousness of the situation, Munley filed a suit requiring Jeter to move.

The case was referred to a federal court judge who had been in the area at the request of the AEC to investigate federal laws governing prosecutions for gambling and the sale of intoxicating liquors. Judge F. M. Brown concurred with the forest officer's account and rendered a mandatory injunction that required Jeter to remove himself and all structures erected by him from the land in question. Upon his failure to do so, the U.S. marshal for the third division would be required to bodily remove the defendant and his belongings. At last, when Jeter was finally out of the way, Mears and Christensen were free to proceed with their plans—but not for long.


## QUESTION OF AMENITIES

By the end of July 1915, nineteen railroad contracts had been let, many for the clearing of land for the townsite. Others were for grading near the new warehouse, laying a wood-stave water line, transporting feed for horses, painting, ditching, and building wagon roads. In the interest of maintaining the momentum of the work, Mears and Christensen tried to keep a comfortable distance between themselves and the townspeople. Even so, the residents continued to rely heavily upon Mears for counsel and advice. Many industrious individuals sank wells on their own properties, but the majority of people wanted to know when the AEC would replace the temporary water system and provide them with electricity and sewers. They were not ready to tax or incorporate themselves and were content to let the commission take care of them.

Relief came when U.S. Comptroller General John R. McCarl authorized the expenditure of AEC funds for a 100,000-gallon water tank for the townsite. At the same time, foreseeing the future need for another water tank of equal capacity, Mears notified Chairman Edes that sooner or later they would have to approach McCarl again with a similar request. Additional funds from the AEC's appropriation would have to be used to cover the needs of the town that had grown beyond anyone's wildest imagination. Granted, the commission was responsible for helping to establish communities along the railbelt, but the requirements of the Ship Creek populace had surpassed all expectations.

Furthermore, although land had been set aside for a schoolhouse, no provision was in place to finance the project or, for

*Photo by Crittenden*

As first president of the Anchorage Woman's Club, Jane Mears spearheaded the effort to build a school for the town. Known today as the Pioneer School, this building was completed in 1915 and relocated to its present site in 1965.

that matter, to educate the children who continued to arrive with the spouses of the workers. Concerned local women sought assistance from Mears' wife. Jane was president of the newly formed Anchorage Woman's Club, dedicated to public education. With school-age children of her own, she understood their plight and prevailed upon her husband to help the townspeople acquire a school. Now it was Mears' turn to cut the red tape. With the help of Chairman Edes and Comptroller McCarl's liberal interpretation of the AEC's powers, Mears received authority to allow the citizens to build a school for ninety pupils. Funded in part by the residents of the town, in-kind labor, the Anchorage Woman's Club, and a small grant from the territorial government, the school was completed in November of 1915.

## TOWN NAME—A TOSS UP

The official naming of the new townsite involved a multi-tude of players including the local chamber of commerce, Alaska's Governor, the Secretary of Interior, the *Cook Inlet Pioneer*, the townspeople, and Mears. Anchorage had other identities, even though the U.S. Post Office gave it that name at the beginning of the railroad project. When large ships first dropped anchor in the waters off shore at Old Knik, the general area was referred to as Knik Anchorage. Then, after Mears set up the construction camp, it became known as Ship Creek.

On July 16, 1915, territorial Governor John F. A. Strong presented the residents with a resolution to change the name of their town and post office to a "name with more significance and local association." People were perplexed by the governor's suggestion because they had expected to have a say in the matter. As before, they asked Mears for guidance. In his best diplomatic form, he explained that the governor had proposed the name of Matanuska because of the new town's geological location relative to the coal fields. He assured the residents that he would be pleased to suggest the new name to the proper authorities if it met with their approval.

Not everyone agreed. A great many businessmen and representatives of the chamber of commerce who thought it would be a mistake to change the name held an election to give citizens an opportunity to decide the issue themselves. According to the *Cook Inlet Pioneer*, nine names were on the ballot. A certificate of the election two weeks later indicated that of the 535 votes cast, the winner was Alaska City, with 146 votes. The runners-up were: Lane-129, Anchorage-101, and Matanuska-54.

Two and a half months later, in consultation by wire with Edes in Seward, Mears stressed that it had seemed prudent not to take immediate action because a number of residents and businessmen had reservations about the name change. Also a recent cable from Lane indicated he thought it best to keep the name of Anchorage for the present. The issue evolved naturally, regardless of Strong's wishes. From the time of its inception, the town of Anchorage had already become more widely known by that name than any other, and it was too late to do anything more about changing it.

## PROGRESS DERAILED

In the dark days of winter, when the ground was frozen solid and a foot of snow lay on the earth, the commission's land office continued to open new additions to the Anchorage townsite for those who wanted to purchase more lots and tracts. By then, about seven miles of road had been laid out.

Although the commissioners' first several months in Alaska were largely taken up with other demands, overall railroad construction efforts, remarkably, were progressing ahead of schedule. In Seward, negotiations were underway for the purchase of the Alaska Northern Railroad and its properties. The southern division under Edes' direction had already undertaken some railroad reconstruction and had put the roadway into shape for gas-car traffic as far as mile 53 out of Seward. In Riggs' northern division, survey parties had staked out nearly 165 miles of railroad location between Broad Pass and Fairbanks. He and his assistants also had evaluated the Tanana Valley Railroad and accompanying properties for possible purchase by the AEC. To expedite matters, the commission set up its executive organization with Edes as president, Mears as vice-president, and chief accountant Burton H. Barndollar as secretary and treasurer.

The AEC's accomplishments to date were impressive, but, toward the end of 1915, the commission had spent the year's appropriation of $1 million in six months. As a result, for all practical purposes, the work had ceased. Caught without sufficient funds, the commissioners were forced to ask Secretary Lane for an emergency appropriation of $2 million to enable them to continue the project through the winter. Lane, however, could not comprehend why or how the work would proceed during that time of year. What better time to slow down the pace? Dreamer that he was, he had apparently forgotten urging his commissioners to push the work aggressively toward the Matanuska coal fields.

Lane's sudden reversal put Mears in a quandary. He was not ready to lay off his work force and was eager to forge ahead. The ten days he'd recently spent inspecting the Matanuska branch line area had been a revelation. There would be tremendous practical advantage to hauling freight in the winter when the Matanuska River became a highway of ice. To his mind, the cost of transporting railroad construction materials over wet, spongy trails in the summer should not even be considered.

Exasperated, Mears sent a strongly worded letter to Lane hoping to expand the secretary's understanding of the situation:

> I haven't any particular desire to go to the penitentiary for statutory embezzlement in overrunning our appropriation; neither have I any desire to sit down on the job with my hands folded for seven months of the year. There are 400 or 500 laborers in camp now, near the Anchorage townsite, all entirely idle. There is no good reason why the work should not go ahead actively. There will probably never be a better time to secure good labor so easily.

Edes again joined forces with Mears in urging Lane to support the AEC's emergency appropriation. How did the commissioners fare as they waited for decisions from Washington? Riggs summed it up well when he said, "We've got to get along and scheme along and lend and borrow the best we can. . . ."

*Mears collection*
Artist Sydney Laurence photographed Anchorage as it appeared in January 1916.

## BALLAINE'S ANTAGONISM

Concurrent with these appeals, opposing forces were also in contact with Lane. One of those was John Ballaine, who had been sorely defeated in his plan to make millions out of his real estate holdings in Seward. When it was first thought that Seward might be the construction base for the railroad, people had rushed there to line up for work and property. But, when they learned that Ship Creek had been chosen instead, they quickly abandoned Seward for the new townsite. Although the AEC had made an effort to include Seward in its planning through the purchase of the Alaska Northern Railroad, Ballaine was not satisfied. It was plain to him that he and the town had lost out.

*Seattle Argus*
John E. Ballaine —Holding his Alaska Central Railway in one hand, John Ballaine is shown standing on Seward, Alaska, the town he and his brother Frank Ballaine founded in 1903. The line experienced many years of financial problems until the Alaska Railroad purchased it in 1915.

In an intense vendetta against the commission, he wrote, published, and circulated letters, memos, and articles intended to confuse the public and taint the government's project in Alaska. Christensen's December report to his boss, Clay Tallman, for example, included a November 8, 1915, story that Ballaine had concocted out of his lucid imagination for the *Alaska Weekly Post* to lead anyone to believe a conspiracy was afoot to change the route of the railroad. Copies of his embellished article and other equally misleading pieces were sent regularly to the Alaska Bureau of the Seattle Chamber of Commerce and to congressmen from California and New York.

Ballaine went to great lengths to prove his credibility, representing fiction as fact whenever necessary. An example of his artifice surfaced when he reportedly sat down at a typewriter in the office of Bernard Stone, his current editor for the *Seward Gateway*, and wrote out a bogus telegram from Seattle, dated December 13, 1915, hinting that there was a movement astir in the state of Washington to urge John Ballaine to run for U.S. Senate. To Ballaine's chagrin, Stone refused to publish it.

In spite of these efforts to undermine the work of the AEC, it seemed clear to Lane that the government had been justified in choosing Ship Creek for its terminal operations because it already owned the land there. Further, the area's fortuitous location close to the Matanuska coal fields assured considerable savings in transportation costs. Still, Ballaine's criticisms of the project had so unnerved the secretary that he decided to delay action on the commission's emergency request in order to reevaluate the conflicting reports before him.

The Alaska Railroad was not in as advantageous a position with Congress as the Panama Canal had been. Most legislators had never been to Alaska, and it was difficult for them to comprehend the rigors and demands of rail construction there. The same also held true for Lane: astute as he may have been, he was ahead of his time in his ambitions for development of a territory he had not seen firsthand. He expected the commission to perform miracles, and when those failed to materialize, he began to question where the work in Alaska was going.

Back in October, Ballaine had informed Christensen that Lane was worried over complaints he'd heard from people in Anchorage who felt the lots they were paying for had been misrepresented during the land sale. He stated further that he was trying to persuade the president and Lane not to spend any more money in Anchorage because a harbor there was not feasible and coal was lacking. Unshaken, Christensen wrote Tallman that through the years he'd had the opportunity to get well acquainted with Ballaine, and that he found him to be about the most unreliable man he'd ever met.

Tallman sent Christensen's memo to Lane. After reading it in context with the correspondence from Edes and Mears, the secretary put aside all thoughts of postponing the AEC's funding request and determined instead to approve the appropriation directly. President Wilson also gave his "earnest approval," as did W. G. McAdoo, Secretary of the Treasury. By then, Lane had sufficient grounds to seek concurrence from John J. Fitzgerald, Chairman of the House Committee on Appropriations. But daylight in Alaska had reached its minimum, and winter cold was at its peak. The process seemed interminable.

That same December, Mears had one further demand on his attention—a happy one he could share with his whole family. On Christmas day, in the AEC's log hospital on the snow flats of Ship Creek, Jane gave birth to the couple's third child, a boy. Lieutenant Mears had prevailed through a year of discovery, frustration, triumph, and unexpected developments at every turn, and he had reason enough to be satisfied. But the arrival of his son, Frederick Mears III, made him deeply proud.

*Mears collection*

Mears' daughters, Jo (left) and Betty (right) with Jane holding Frederick Mears III, born December 25, 1915.

## CHAPTER 8

# SIDETRACKED BY SKIRMISHES

*Face every task with a determination to conquer its
difficulties and to never let them conquer you.*

Colonel G. W. Goethals

Some of the most sluggish and back-breaking work during
the early phase of the project took place along Turnagain Arm, a
narrow extension of Cook Inlet. This name evolved naturally in
1778, when Captain Cook realized he would have to turn his ship
around again because the arm did not lead through. Situated in a
fjord-like setting where mountains directly abut the sea, the waterway is a place of wildflowers and waterfalls in summer. In winter,
though, warm chinook winds often surround the steep terrain, dis-

charging massive avalanches of snow, rock, and uprooted trees onto the railroad right-of-way.

When the *Seattle Sunday Times* heralded, "Uncle Sam's Iron Men Open Up Alaska" in January 1916, repercussions from any setbacks, major or minor, were left out of the equation. The article estimated another three or four years before Mears, punching rails along Turnagain Arm and up through the Susitna Valley, would meet Riggs, pushing his way from the opposite direction, at a midpoint somewhere in the wilds of Alaska. This forecast would prove to be overly optimistic.

## CANNON FIRES FIRST ROUND

Back in the capital, chairman Edes stood firm. He had been called before the House Committee on Territories to defend the AEC's $2 million emergency funding request. With facts and figures well in hand, the studious man was prepared to address major items of concern: the Matanuska Valley work and the installation within that area of a branch line to the Chickaloon coal fields; the grading of the new line north to Talkeetna; and the 45-mile extension of the line from Ship Creek south to Kern Creek. California congressman Charles F. Curry, chairman of the House Committee on Territories and a vocal supporter of the railroad, moderated the hearings. The proceedings were dominated, however, by Illinois congressman Joe Cannon, a staunch friend and ally of John Ballaine.

From the start, it was obvious to Curry that Cannon had been coached to sidetrack Edes into discussing issues of particular importance to Ballaine instead of those on the agenda. He wanted to know, for instance, exactly when the connection between Ship Creek and Kern Creek would be made and precisely when the renovated rolling stock of the Alaska Northern would be ready for service.

Somewhat annoyed, but completely sure of himself, Edes explained that construction in that section of the project would take at least twelve or fifteen months due to the threat of avalanches and the slow work of carving a roadbed out of solid rock. Edes' detailed knowledge of the undertaking made it indisputably clear that, unless the necessary funds became available, the commission's schedule would be delayed for almost a full year. Later Edes was heard to remark off the record, "Umph! It'll take so many cubic yards of excavation and so many millions of dollars, and that's all there is to it."

It was a close call, but at the end of February, Congress finally awarded the $2 million for continuing the commission's work. Committee members who favored the appropriation had prevailed—by three votes—over Cannon's vigorous opposition. After clearing this obstacle, however, the commissioners soon found they were having to pay higher prices for materials and freight. Their problems were far from over.

In Anchorage, conditions in and around the terminal area were anything but safe. In order to protect those using the utilities of the railroad, Mears posted advisory notices about town. Topics ran from harbor improvements, railway travel, flag stops, and freight shipments, to conservation of water and electricity, care of the injured, and directives against using gasoline or alcohol for heating.

Despite Mears' attempts to keep liquor out of the town, it had found its way in, courtesy of a licensed saloon at Knik. Then, too, school enrollment had doubled, forcing teachers to work in overcrowded classrooms. A new school would have to be built.

Without question, Mears was overworked, but in April 1916, relief was in sight. With the concurrence of Secretary Lane, Chairman Edes established a Land and Industrial Department to oversee matters outside the sphere of railroad engineering and construction. He appointed Andrew Christensen manager of the new department and director of the school.

## RESURGENCE THWARTED

One of Mears' major concerns was for the comfort and well-being of his men. Without their cooperation, his efforts would have been for naught. Wanting to keep as many as possible working, he adopted a familiar system that had been used in railroad construction throughout the West. Under this plan, private contractors were responsible for clearing, grubbing, and grading the railroad right-of-way in 100-foot segments known as "stations."

These station men were a diverse lot, made up of Russians, Greeks, Italians, Germans, and some Scandinavians. Working together in small groups, they usually took on several stations at a time for a certain price per cubic yard or per acre. In the interest of economy, those hired were asked to provide whatever basic tools they themselves could supply for the job. Dressed in rough weather gear, rubber galoshes or leather boots, and hats shrouded in mosquito netting, the men put in long, somber hours chopping, shoveling, and hauling. Understanding their pay would be dependent upon the amount of work accomplished, each of the station men had an incentive to exert his best efforts.

Mears also did everything in his power to maintain good labor relations among the commission's employees. When in the field, he took time to converse with the men and commend them for jobs well done. When construction differences got out of hand, he would mount his horse or ride the train out on the line to resolve them. Yet, despite fair warning that all jobs had been filled, countless unemployed men stood about with nothing to do and nowhere to go. Taking advantage of the situation, agitators from Seward began to infiltrate Anchorage, creating unrest and skepticism about the AEC's employment practices. A series of small strikes followed in February and resulted in formation of the Alaska Federal Labor Union.

The complaint centered on an 1892 law that prohibited federal employees, or laborers assigned to federally sponsored projects, from working more than an eight-hour day. Claiming the AEC was

Mears willingly took time to confer with engineers and workers at distant construction camps.

operating in violation of that law, the hastily organized union called out its teamsters and effectively shut down construction in the Anchorage division. Not about to be bullied, Mears wired Lane to send troops to provide safe conduct for men willing to stay on the job. He knew from his own railroad experience that the 1892 law did not apply to transportation projects. He was fully within his rights in giving his men nine or ten hours of work a day, and the option of taking on other small tasks up to eleven or twelve hours. To back his position he cabled Edes:

> Every railroad in the country handled its business in accordance with an Interstate Commerce Commission ruling: that train crews on any project shall not work more than 16 hours without having four hours' rest. . . . If the Alaska work is held down by the eight-hour law it will result in some very costly operating expenses, and we will be the laughing stock of the entire railroad world.

Instead of dispatching troops to Alaska as Mears had wanted, Lane asked William B. Wilson, Secretary of Labor, to send a conciliation committee to the territory. The panel was to take testimony and establish a new wage schedule. As this committee gathered affidavits, the union called another general strike. This one was so well coordinated that ninety percent of the terminal employees were off the job during the first afternoon. Four days later, a determined Mears hired independent station men to take their places.

Realizing that the chief engineer was administering the work in Alaska almost singlehandedly, Lane called a meeting of cabinet officers who committed themselves to swift and decisive action. He informed Mears directly that forty troops were rushing to Anchorage aboard a revenue cutter from Valdez. He also sent a district judge to swear in as many additional men as were needed for the work.

Lane's labor contingent completed its investigations by the end of April, going out of its way to support Mears, even to the extent of raising his recommended wage scale of 37.5 cents per hour to 40 cents. With the settlement of the strike, the AEC workers returned safely to their jobs and Lane's troops, who had provided security for a short time, went on to other assignments.

## HORSES, CRANES, AND A STERN-WHEEL BOAT

By now, Edes was spending most of his time in Washington. The engineer-in-charge at Seward was R. J. Weir, a former engineer for the Southern Pacific Railroad, who coordinated with Mears in supervising the repair of the rolling stock and railbed acquired from the Alaska Northern. Their goal to have it in working condition by the summer of 1916 proved to be another massive undertaking. Track installed too low was to be raised and reinforced with thousands of yards of gravel ballast and new crossties. Miles of abandoned trestles also needed to be replaced. All of these tasks took

A.E.C. 39 *Track laid across swamp on logs.*

*Mears collection*

Tracks laid across the swamps on logs.

much longer than expected. It would be nearly October before a train consisting of a 60-ton engine, a caboose, and a few light cars could operate from Seward to Kern Creek.

In charge of the construction of 230 miles of main line himself, Mears oversaw delivery of hundreds of tons of railroad materials and supplies that arrived by steamer: locomotives, derricks, bridge-timbers, structural steel, and boilers. Horses, too, were an integral part of the cargo and were always the first to be offloaded by crane. One by one, they were suspended in heavy canvas hammocks and carefully swung onto the decks of barges waiting alongside the ship. Upon landing, they immediately went to work on the front line of duty. Their job was to pull rail flats, filled with the commission's freight, over tracks which the workers had laid directly on the mud between the water's edge and the higher ground of the terminal.

While performing their survey in 1914, the three commissioners had discovered that there was no simple way to pierce the raw land of the interior with a railroad. They did agree, however, that the rail line could parallel the Susitna River for a distance of seventy-five miles upstream from its mouth on Cook Inlet. Undeterred by the shallow waters of the river, Mears and his engineers found they could use their jack-of-all-trades, the *Omineca*, a stern-wheel river boat the commission had purchased from a Canadian railroad company. The vessel was capable of carrying one hundred tons of cargo and men in a single trip up river as far as Kroto. It soon paid for itself in time and labor saved.

Farther north, the engineers designed and built three "river tunnel boats" to ply the numerous gravel-filled channels intersecting the Susitna above Kroto. Drawing only about twenty inches of water when loaded to capacity at thirty tons, these boats transported 2,700 tons of materials and more than a thousand laborers to the construction sites.

*AEC G-513 Anchorage Museum of History and Art*

The stern-wheel boat *Omineca* proved expedient in transporting the AEC's men and materials through the shallow waters of the Susitna River.

By the summer of 1916, the land once occupied by tents had become an expansive railroad marshaling yard and staging area.

Concurrently with this work, crews at Ship Creek were transforming the early construction camp into a railroad headquarters. For materials, they used trees logged from the site and lumber brought in from Knik. In all, the summer of 1916 saw completion of the AEC's office building, a mechanical shop, a warehouse, a dock and freight shed, a power house, a passenger depot, and improved accommodations for employees.

## VISIBLE PROGRESS

During August 1916, Chairman Edes, accompanied by his wife, Mary, returned to Alaska. His mission was to inspect the work accomplished in his absence and to report back to Lane. Upon landing in Seward, he saw first the commission's refurbished headquarters in offices once occupied by managers of the Alaska Northern Railroad. A considerable amount of construction had taken place in the old terminal yard. New sidings had been laid, and an industrial rail spur had been installed along the waterfront to accommodate new businesses and warehouses.

R. J. Weir took the chairman and other railroad officials out on the line north of Seward to inspect the ongoing work. There Edes observed hundreds of men, almost lost in clouds of dust, repairing the roadbed and raising miles of track to allow for proper drainage. Others were restoring the rustic work camps of the old Alaska Northern in preparation for winter.

In Anchorage, Mears gave Edes a broad-brush tour of the branch line to the Matanuska coal fields and of the grading underway just north of Matanuska Junction. On return, he explained how he planned to transport complete outfits and supplies into the construction camps when winter ice stabilized the rivers.

The following day, in a steady downpour, Mears, Edes, and a small crew stuffed themselves into rubberized rain gear and lum-

*William Wilson collection 84-16-18N, Rasmuson Library, University of Alaska Fairbanks*
A washout in the Peter's Creek area 22 miles north of Anchorage, October, 1916.

bered aboard a motorized longboat for an investigation of the turbulent Susitna River. Stopping along the way, the men stepped cautiously onto the rain-soaked banks of the river to scrutinize hazardous areas Mears had identified earlier on his maps. This trip gave Mears an opportunity to explain to Edes how he planned to bridge the Susitna and other rivers beyond.

On a trip farther north, Edes joined Mears and Riggs and a party of engineers to review the heavy work underway in the Nenana River canyon. There, the constant sloughing of earth from the sides of the canyon was proving to be almost as formidable a challenge as the terrain along Turnagain Arm. After evaluating all of the problems facing them in the interior, the three commissioners were forced to admit that difficulties might multiply in the months ahead.

On his way back to the capital, Edes sent a strongly worded message to Lane informing him that the adverse reports about the AEC's operations were coming from those who were disappointed because they had not received a share of the $35 million. "They do not appreciate that the road is being built for the benefit of Alaska and its present population," he wrote. "Opposition will come for a time from our friend Delegate Wickersham and others who have only selfish objects in view, but the sentiment of the best people is with us." Here he named Bishop Peter T. Rowe, Governor Strong of Alaska, and Leopold David, the U.S. Commissioner at Anchorage, all of whom were reliable supporters of the commission's work.

PLOWED UNDER

In the fall of 1916, Mears received official notice of his commission as army captain. This promotion reminded him that his first commitment was to his duty and that he must remain alert to potential problems, whatever form they took.

When he learned from Christensen, for example, that teachers were living without pay and on credit from merchants, he immediately sent a memorandum to Lane requesting action. As before, this was his only recourse in matters beyond his authority. Until now, federal officials had remained unwilling and ill-prepared to accept fiscal responsibility for public education in Anchorage. The territorial government, likewise, was unable to provide school funds for an unincorporated town. Reluctant to spend railroad monies on schooling, Lane nevertheless agreed to advance federal funds temporarily until legislation could be enacted to resolve the issue. A full year would pass before a second school was built and the railroad funds were reimbursed.

In addition, the problem of liquor had yet to be eliminated. When Christensen learned that gambling was running "wide open" at the Montana Pool Hall, he reported it to Mears. In the back rooms of several places around the town, he said, there was some-

*AEC G-551 Anchorage Museum of History and Art*

Gambling paraphernalia and liquor supplies in Anchorage were destroyed in response to Mears' concerns about the town's orderly development and the welfare of its citizens.

*AEC G-1754 Anchorage Museum of History and Art*
Avalanches repeatedly halted work along the railroad route.

times as much as $1,500 in one pot on the table. Fearing the situation would get out of hand this time, Mears petitioned for the transfer of a U.S. district attorney from Valdez to be permanently assigned at Anchorage. In justifying the request, he wrote, "The Alaska Engineering Commission is now employing 3,700 men, all centered on this town, and is disbursing nearly half a million dollars each month. These facts alone should be sufficient to emphasize the importance of this recommendation." After a deputy arrived, AEC crews were directed to confiscate the gambling paraphernalia and haul the liquor in wheelbarrows to Ship Creek. Wielding hammers and axes, they destroyed all evidence that the diversions had ever taken place.

In late October of 1916, P. S. Hunt, photographer for the AEC, recorded one of the most destructive avalanches yet, at mile 53 north of Seward. The slide derailed a train, engulfed the work, and virtually shut down all of the surrounding railroad activity. Remarkably, no one was injured, but the event was a tremendous setback. Remembering the lessons of Panama's Culebra Cut, Mears had to admit that slides would continue and could not be ignored.

*AEC G-1490 Anchorage Museum of History and Art*
Of necessity, fortress-like sheds were built to divert sliding snow and allow safe
passage of trains along Turnagain Arm.


He estimated about 8,000 linear feet of fortress-type sheds, strong
enough to withstand the shock of an unpredictable slide, would
have to be built. Realizing that only time, patience, manpower, and
another season of work would correct the situation, he drew up
schedules for clearing the right-of-way to allow for construction of
the snow sheds. An additional five hundred men had to be hired
for that work. Traffic did not resume for another ten months.


## CONFLICTING OPINIONS IN THE PRESS

Mears stopped at Seward in December 1916, on his way to
Washington, D. C., where he planned to consult with Lane. Newsmen there took the opportunity to pellet him with questions. The

*AEC G-1529 Anchorage Museum of History and Art*

The view on exiting a snow shed, showing enormous walls of snow on either side, obviously carved by the rotary plow.

follow-up article in the *Alaska Weekly Post* carried the headline, "Surprising Delay of U. S. Railroad." When asked whether the commission intended to complete the line through to Fairbanks before opening the road between Seward and Anchorage, Mears retorted, "Absurd, don't you realize that the line cannot be opened to Fairbanks before 1920 or 1921?"

When they wanted to know whether the line along Turnagain Arm would be completed by November 1917, he told them, "It certainly will not, without a real waste of money. It cannot be hurried or completed within that time because of the demands and precision of the work." He informed them that, although the commission had not received its June appropriation, it had been able to push the work as far as Potter Creek. To this he added, "Anyone who contends that we have not used our best efforts on the Turnagain Arm work this year is not in possession of the facts."

A rotary plow was used to clear snow from the tracks.

Pressing him further, the reporters questioned why a harbor was needed at Anchorage—was he aware that one of the Admiral Line boats had touched bottom two or three times on departing Anchorage? Mears replied simply, "The boat was off its course," and ended the interview by stating that he did not plan to become involved in any controversy between Seward and Anchorage. If reporters wanted additional information, he suggested, they should read the Secretary of Interior's report.

A few days later, some folks in Fairbanks injected themselves into the situation, lambasting Mears with claims that he was holding back the construction of the railroad to pull down just that much more salary. Thomas Riggs quickly took up the defense of Mears in a news release from Nenana. His article declared that the reputations of the commissioners depended upon the success of the railroad project. If the work could be completed by the end of another year, it would mean more to them than the salaries they would receive for a longer period of construction.

On December 24, 1916, the *Anchorage Daily Times and Cook Inlet Pioneer* built its own case in defense of Mears, delivering it to

*Mears collection*

Rotary plow at work.

*Mears collection*

Roatary plow imprint in the snow.

him almost as a Christmas present. In its lead story, "Anchorage Coal Terminal," they criticized Seward's *Alaska Weekly Post* for its opposition to the construction of harborage facilities and coal bunkers at the mouth of Ship Creek. They accused the newspaper of garnishing the facts to support its cause and then inflicting questionable calculations upon an unsuspecting public. "The only reward for their efforts," the *Times* claimed, "would be to demonstrate the adage that, while figures do not lie, liars can figure."

Upon reading these accounts, Mears must have been glad to realize there were others who understood what he was up against. No doubt he hoped the new year would bring freedom from further petty entanglements.

## CHAPTER 9

# TRANQUILITY AT HOME—
# TURMOIL ABROAD

*If your future in the engineering world loomed bright before you, would you chuck it all to pursue an ideal?*

Columnist Ashmun Brown
*New York Press*, 1914

What the next months produced were difficulties of a different kind. As the AEC struggled to pry open the northern domain, the nation was preparing for war. Harried legislators, trapped in the vise of urgent demands, were reluctant to advance railroad appropriations as scheduled. The cost of materials, labor, and commodities suddenly began to escalate. Maintaining the momentum of the

Like his mentor John Stevens, Mears often puffed a cigar while he worked in the field.

government project in the face of those setbacks took vigorous, forceful leadership. J. J. Delaney, who joined the project in 1916 and later became general manager of the railroad, recognized that, through it all, Mears was "a man who got things done."

Beyond the strategic planning, the welfare of the workers was of uppermost importance to Mears. On Turnagain Arm alone, more than a thousand men, divided into approximately fifty station gangs, worked summer and winter along its precarious slopes. With dynamite they blasted some 75,000 cubic yards of rock from the area. Horses hauled away the spoil on small, flat-bed trolleys to storage areas where the rock would be crushed and used for fill as needed. All of this work was toilsome and hazardous. Collisions, derailments, and accidents on the job occurred regularly, resulting in death or injury to several hundreds of workers over the course of the project.

Small dispensaries were built at the major construction camps along the line to treat men with minor wounds. The more seriously injured were taken to the larger, 50-bed hospital in Anchorage. When the structure was still in the design stage, Mears had stipulated that it be oriented to provide as much light and sunshine as possible for the well-being of the patients. Built at a cost of $35,000, the facility was considered to be the largest and best equipped building of its kind in the territory.

The chief engineer's leadership style reveals itself further in an incident recounted in the *Washington Evening Star* some years after it occurred:

> My informant with seven others was "mushing," or walking, from the end of steel to one of the camps up in the unfinished section of the line. The going was heavy, and at suppertime they were very tired. Arriving at one of the government camps (these were four to eight miles apart), the weary pedestrians paused in front of the timekeeper's cabin. The timekeeper, who is camp

boss, was in front of the cabin conversing with Mears, who had just arrived on horseback unattended. As he saw the party come to a halt, the timekeeper remarked: "Just keep right on walking, boys; we have no room for you here tonight; it is only a few miles to the next camp." Then turning to Mears, he added, "There is just one unoccupied bed in this camp and you will occupy that."

"Like hell I will," snapped the commissioner. "When you have found beds for everyone of these men it will be time enough to think about me. These men are in here on foot to help us, and they are going to have decent treatment!"

The effect was magical. In twenty minutes beds were extemporized for all. And after that, the timekeeper went from one to another inquiring, "Are you sure you have blankets enough?"

## BREATHING SPACE

At work, Mears maintained a no-nonsense demeanor, focusing his energy upon the task at hand. But, in the privacy of his own home, family and close friends took pleasure in his sharp wit and subtle humor. Out on the job, he could take refuge in Alaska's breathtaking scenery to give perspective to his concerns. An experienced hunter and fisherman, he welcomed every opportunity to enjoy the wilds of the territory, whether riding on horseback, hiking across the tundra, or sleeping on spruce boughs in the shelter of a tent. On those outings, he and those who accompanied him followed the practice of taking no more game than they could preserve or eat in a season.

Summer's late evening daylight gave Mears a chance to toss an occasional lure into the nearest stream. By the campfire, with

pencil and notepad in hand, he might jot a verse or two about his
favorite pastime:

## OUT FISHING

A fellow isn't thinking mean, out fishing!
His thoughts are mostly good and clean, out fishing,
He doesn't knock his fellow men,
Or harbor any grudges then;
A fellow's at his finest when out fishing.

A feller has no time for hate, out fishing.
He isn't eager to be great, out fishing.
He isn't thinking thoughts of self, out fishing,
But he is always just himself, out fishing.

*Mears collection*

"A fellow's . . . always just himself, out fishing," wrote Mears (right).

*Mears collection*

Mears and companion with Dall sheep trophies.

Sometimes Mears hunted for mountain sheep with Morris Marino, then the most famous hunting guide in Alaska. On one of those trips, both men were injured in an accident. As the story goes, Mears cut his leg but somehow managed to sew up the wound by himself. Then, wearing snowshoes, he carried Marino on his back to the nearest camp for treatment. From then on, his family considered him to be a real sourdough in the most rugged Alaska tradition.

For her part, Jane spared no effort in creating a comfortable, if cramped, home life on what today is known as Government Hill. Completion of their new house took time because Mears, who chose to supervise its construction, was frequently away. Finally, during the snapping cold of January 1917, all of the Mearses bundled themselves together in the family sleigh, with as many household items as they could fit in about them, and moved out of AEC Cottage

No. 6. Mears at the reins carefully guided his team of dapple-grays from the north bluff across the flats of Ship Creek and up C Street hill toward West Second Avenue to AEC House No. 29. The two-story residence overlooked Cook Inlet, the terminal yards and the harbor. Directly to the east, stood a row of equally substantial dwellings built for others on the AEC management team.

Anchorage pioneer builder Cappy Faroe observed years later, "Nothing was spared when those structures went up. They had copper boilers, fireplaces, leaded windows and front verandas." In anticipation of the long winters ahead, Mears reasoned that his directors would be more inclined to remain on the job if they were comfortably housed. That group of homes, initially called "Railroad Row," became the vortex of Anchorage's social life. Elsewhere the neighborhood was sometimes dubbed "Silk Stocking Lane." Later, as other houses were added to the area, picture post cards captioned it, "Anchorage's first residence district."

*Mears collection*

AEC House No. 29 was built to Mears' specifications in 1916 and remained his family home until he left Alaska.

Mears with his favorite hunting companion, Curly.

The couple furnished their home in the tradition of the times, with oriental carpets, silver tea service, and heirloom quilts and linens. Mears' hunting trophies hung on walls alongside paintings by a friend, Alaska's foremost artist Sydney Laurence. The place offered a warm and welcome retreat for visiting relatives and officials who often stayed with them for several days at a time.

Household pets were always around. The girls kept two kittens, Boots and Kitty Face. Their father had three hunting dogs: Curly, the retriever, an Airedale named Pat, and an Irish setter. One year, Mears built a pen for two orphaned black bear cubs who had wandered into the yard. After they began to grow, they suddenly disappeared, much to the disappointment of the youngsters.

Growing up in Anchorage was a stimulating experience for the children, disciplined though they were. In those days, according to Betty, "You did whatever your parents told you to do." The ever-present snow was no deterrent to outdoor winter activities, and Mears, who never lost his boyhood sense of fun, welcomed the

*Mears collection*

Mears' own dapple gray horses pull a Christmas tree home for the holidays. Daughter Jo Mears stands next to the sleigh.

Educated in fine arts and music, Jane Mears inspired community participation in musical and theatrical performances.

season. Hitching the dogs to a sled, he would take his children and their friends for whirlwind rides through the neighborhood. On warm summer days, the family would join others for a swim in Lake Spenard. Railroad excursions north to the "Mat" valley and south to Campbell and Rabbit creeks, were popular weekend diversions. Everyone in town was an amateur baseball fan. Stiff competition prevailed between the "Reds" (the YMCA and employees of the AEC) and the "Blues" (staff from the local newspaper and members of the Presbyterian Church).

Having lived in the cosmopolitan Canal Zone and in the nation's capital before coming to Alaska, the lieutenant and his wife brought a touch of refinement to the otherwise isolated frontier town. In contrast to her husband's reserve, Jane was an energetic young woman who devoted herself to the growing community. As first president of the Anchorage Woman's Club, she urged its members to promote scholastic achievement among the school children. With her background in music and voice, she often held rehearsals for local musicals and theatricals in her living room, accompanying them from her Steinway piano. These performances formed the beginnings of cultural activity in the new town.

Jane's February 14 birthday always called for a special celebration. More than once, Mears helped the children make a trail of cut-out red hearts leading from their mother's bedside to a pile of gifts in the parlor. Revealing his more romantic side, he wrote a poem for her each year: "A little love is none at all/that wanders or that fears/A hearty love dwells still at call/to kisses or to tears."

Long after Mears' death, Jane reminisced that her husband had said he cared most of all for her when his eyes met her weary gaze after she'd stayed up through the night with a sick child. Indeed, he cherished first his family and then his books, which he always read with an atlas close by.

Robust though he was, Mears extended himself beyond his endurance toward the end of that winter. A serious bout of pneumonia took him off the job for a number of weeks during that period. Recuperating in the comfort of the family's new home, he had time to reflect on the accomplishments of the previous year and to consider the prospects for 1917. So far, the AEC had established four new townsites on the rail line. Slow but resolute progress continued in Anchorage, along Turnagain Arm, and toward the Matanuska and Nenana coal deposits. In addition, the recently installed permanent wire station on Government Hill above the terminal yards now greatly extended the commission's connection with the outside world. One of the first messages the Mearses sent over the wire was to announce the birth of their fourth child, Helen Rogers Mears, born in Anchorage on April 13, 1917.

The news from abroad, however, grew ever more disturbing. For three years, the major powers of Europe had been fighting, and the conflict was expanding at an alarming rate. Baby Helen's arrival occurred directly on the heels of the president's declaration that America was at war.

## COAL: A WEIGHTY MATTER

When the United States entered World War I, the need for coal and fuel across the nation propelled Alaska into the limelight. Frances S. Peabody, director of the National Council of Defense, urged the Senate Committee on Public Lands to encourage the leasing and mining of coal in the territory. He was convinced the war could be won only if sufficient coal or other fuel were furnished by the United States.

As a military man, Mears could well understand the importance of securing Alaska coal for defense purposes. From the beginning of the project, that goal was the primary reason the 38-mile branch line from Matanuska Junction to the 1,400-acre Chickaloon coal field had been a priority. Even so, the mining and transportation of coal, other than for the AEC's own use, were not explicit functions of the commission nor had Congress appropriated funds for such activity.

*J&T No. 1   Anchorage Museum of History and Art*
Coal seams near the Healy area.

When the AEC first needed coal, workers packed it out on bobsleds and by dog team from a small mine located one-half mile from the Matanuska branch of the railroad at Moose Creek. Before securing coal from this mine at $6 a ton, the commission had been paying about $16 per ton for coal from the Puget Sound area, a situation which had greatly overtaxed the available funds. Later, as construction progressed, the commission made a contractual agreement with a mine operator at Eska and detailed some of its own crews to work there to keep the railroad supplied.

Now, as Peabody pointed out, the need was urgent for a coal port at tidewater on the Pacific to supply fuel to naval ships on patrol. Suddenly the focus turned to Alaska. Conclusive tests had proven the coal in the Matanuska area to be suitable for use by the U.S. Navy. An Anchorage Chamber of Commerce bulletin claimed

that mining the coal field promised a bright future development
from which Anchorage would greatly benefit.

The fact of the matter was, however, that a much larger mining operation than currently existed would have to be established
to meet the navy's requirements, and equipment for building it would
have to be brought in by rail. Not until completion of the branch
line to the Matanuska field would the AEC be in a position to coor-
dinate mining activity with the navy. It would take two more years,
but eventually the cooperative venture paid off when the navy began loading coal from its Chickaloon mine onto Pacific fleet vessels at Anchorage.

## THE QUESTION OF PORT FACILITIES

Beyond the complexities of obtaining coal was the issue of
port facilities. Much to the dismay of Seward's promoters, any coal
that might be available for shipping had no way to get to their town
for at least another year. A formidable amount of work remained
before the Turnagain Arm section of the line from Anchorage to
Seward would be open for traffic. Moreover, some older stretches
of the line near Seward, unstable and especially treacherous in winter, were in constant need of repair.

At Ship Creek, Mears' floating dock had performed yeoman's
service, but it was only a temporary structure. Two years of batter-
ing by broken ice and the ebb and flow of Cook Inlet's 30-foot
tides had rendered it inadequate for handling the anticipated loads.
The interplay of all of these circumstances prompted another round
of rivalry between the two coastal towns.

During the early months of 1917, for purely practical reasons,
the AEC relocated its Seward headquarters, including Edes' offices,
to Anchorage. Certainly the transition would put them in closer
touch with the major construction work. It also would relieve the
AEC from paying the excessively high prices Seward townsite prop-

erty owner John Ballaine was asking for lots the commission had been considering for expansion. As a result, many Seward residents moved to Anchorage for the sake of holding on to their railroad jobs or finding new employment.

Seward's business officials did not take kindly to the exodus of its townspeople to Anchorage, and their resentment intensified. They asked Josephus Daniels, then Secretary of the Navy and a new convert of Ballaine's, to convince Secretary Lane that Seward's harbor would be preferable as a coaling base because it was open all year long. In his letter to Lane, Daniels said that Anchorage could not be considered an open harbor because some months of the year it was closed by ice. He pressed for expeditious completion of the line connecting Seward to Ship Creek and the coal fields.

Several months before, however, chairman Edes had sent an urgent memo to Lane pointing out that he was not about to risk his professional reputation by recommending an additional 115-mile heavy railway haul of coal from Anchorage over the fragile grades to Seward. In his view, unless sufficient funds were made available to the AEC for building a shipping point at Anchorage, the entire railroad venture would never be a success. Further, he stressed the importance of letting dredging contracts for the next season's work or at the very least allowing the commission to build the necessary dredge at Ship Creek. Lane mulled over the advantages and disadvantages of both harbors. Already overburdened with urgent concerns related to the war, he vacillated on the subject for an uncharacteristically long time and postponed issuing any directives.

From Mears' point of view, the dredging and building of an adequate port at Anchorage had always been integral to the railroad project. Indeed, the railroad's enabling legislation had required the AEC to take steps to open coal fields within close proximity of the rail corridor. In his estimation, Anchorage was the logical location for the rail terminal. It offered the shortest distance between coal fields and tidewater, as well as the best flat grade for transporting the heavy freight.

Routine arrival of steamships from Panama, loaded to the guards with railroad machinery, underscored the imperative to replace Mears' original dock. Although the spectacle of discharging the cumbersome cargo provided entertainment for the townspeople, the job itself was a tremendous ordeal. In late April, for instance, the vessel *Turret Crown*, towing the barge *St. David* stacked with dump cars, flat-bed car bodies, and thirteen locomotives, had to anchor off shore in Cook Inlet. Powerful locomotive cranes lifted that machinery from the barge and carefully placed it all onto the decks of the "mosquito fleet." These were the smaller barges and launches from Knik which the AEC enlisted to lighter everything to shore.

From the time of his first arrival, Mears had known that larger ships would never be able to approach the shores of Anchorage, even during high tides, until the creek was enlarged and

*William Wilson collection 84-16-20N, Rasmuson Library, University of Alaska Fairbanks*
Cranes offloaded locomotives, other heavy machinery and even horses from vessels arriving at the Anchorage harbor.

a serviceable dock installed. Clearly, dredging was the expedient thing to do now, especially since the U.S. Navy planned to build a mine in the Matanuska coal field. With all of these considerations in mind, Mears decided to proceed on the course that made the most sense to him, despite Lane's reservations.

Through his Panama connections, he hired William Gerig to implement the AEC's plans. A trim, scholarly sort of man with a graying Vandyke beard, Gerig was an engineer of considerable repute. On similar projects elsewhere, he had designed dredging equipment which he believed would serve equally well in this case. In his opinion, the wharf envisioned by Mears could be maintained and vessels would be able to reach it practically all year round.

In the interest of economy, the plan was to outfit the commission's 140-foot barge, the *Sperm*, with dredging equipment. Commission crews set up an electric plant on the barge and organized the storage of about one-half mile of floating and shore-discharge pipe. Under Gerig's supervision, they installed an engine, a centrifugal pump and two boilers. A powerful cutter head had the capability of excavating clay and harder materials to a depth of seventy-five feet. In full operation, the dredge could remove 150,000 cubic yards of sand per month. Gerig estimated that, once the new 800-foot wharf was in place, including the railroad and wagon road approaches, it would have capacity for handling 1,500 to 2,000 tons of coal per day.

Wanting Gerig to be able to complete the work without accident or interference, Mears closed the port to navigation for the winter. In a memo to Edes, he justified his decision citing the demands of previous seasons in lightering heavy freight through the ice, with steam tugs of inadequate power. He expected the harbor improvements would be ready for traffic by the fall of 1918. One challenge for the engineers would be to build embankments strong enough to deflect floating ice away from the face of the new dock. This was a problem Gerig would have to address in his design.

The chief engineer out on the line.

Meanwhile, work on the Matanuska branch line continued at its own pace. On October 14, 1917, the first train ran through to the end of the line at Chickaloon, a distance of 74 miles from Anchorage. A week later, the first shipment of Matanuska coal from a unit on the Chickaloon River arrived in Anchorage. The load consisted of 60 tons, and all of it was used as fuel for railroad construction activities. The event marked an important milestone in the progress of the project.

## A SOLDIER'S DUTY

The United States had remained neutral during President Wilson's efforts to reach a peaceful settlement of the world conflict, and Alaska's distance from the U.S. border had insulated the territory from direct involvement in the hostilities. But finally, on April 2, 1917, Wilson declared war against Germany. "The day has come," he said, "when America is privileged to spend her might for the principles that gave her birth. . . . I am not now thinking of the loss of property involved. . .property can be paid for; the lives of peaceful and innocent people cannot be." Then the seriousness of the situation touched everyone—especially patriots like Mears.

Newspapers dramatized the intensity of the conflict in banner headlines; Lane was quoted in a speech saying, "Feudalism is making its last stand against oncoming democracy. . . .This is a war to save America, to preserve self-respect, to justify our right to live." All men of military standing, including those not in active service, were expected to step forward.

It was a painful dilemma for Mears, torn as he was between his loyalties to his wife and growing family, to the railroad he had worked so hard for, and to his country. Although he considered the war with Germany a just war, the entire spectacle gave Mears many a sleepless night. He had every confidence the railroad could be built in his absence by capable engineers who wanted to see it completed, but he had yet to come to grips about what he himself should do. On the day he made his decision, Betty watched her father pace fretfully back and forth across the living room. Finally, heaving a long sigh, he turned to his wife and grasped her shoulders. "Johnnie," he said, "I could never face my children if I didn't go."

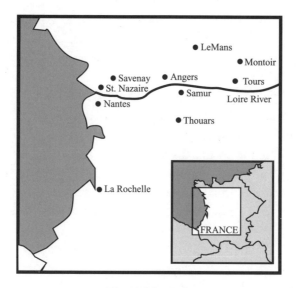

**CHAPTER 10**

# OFF TO WAR

*With our backs to the wall, and believing in the justice of our cause, each one of us must fight to the end.*

British Commander General Douglas Haig,
France 1915-18

Late in November 1917, Commissioner Mears received from the Department of War his promotion to the rank of major. This news confirmed the decision he had struggled with to return to active military service. The orders he was given were urgent and demanding. One of the pressing questions at the time was whether the U.S. could train and equip an army and ship it to France in time to stem the tide of the German advance. Mears was to recruit a regiment of approximately 1,000 men for the construction and operation of American military rail lines in France. Taking immediate charge, he sought and was given Lane's authorization to solicit employees of the AEC for his regiment.

To some Mears' departure from Alaska may have seemed abrupt, but it was not taken in haste. To the extent he could, he detailed the remaining work so that construction would continue toward completion in his absence. Christensen agreed to serve as manager in his place. Even so, the war would seriously hamper progress on the railroad. In fact, the AEC's work force shrank to half when many employees lined up to join Mears or left to seek more lucrative work in the States.

## TOWNSPEOPLE BID FAREWELL

With news of the Mearses' imminent departure, the town held a gala farewell banquet and reception on January 3, 1918, in the Anchorage Labor Temple. American flags and yards of red, white, and blue bunting festooned the auditorium and tables. As the dinner progressed, the couple received small personal gifts of gold, ivory, and jade. Speakers commended Mears for the legacy he would leave in the form of a well-built town and Jane for her contributions to the educational and social growth of the community.

Andrew Christensen praised Mears as a "man of action—an executive who accomplished things—who would have done much more had not limitations been placed upon his appropriations." Then, by proxy, he presented Mears with a photograph of two cavalry sabers. One was for duty in the field. The second, for dress, was etched in gold and bore an ivory handle. The initials "FM," embedded in diamonds, adorned the front of the hilt. Employees and associates of the Alaska Engineering Commission wanted Mears to treasure the sabers as mementos of his ties to them and the years he'd spent in Anchorage. Having been unable to secure the swords locally, Christensen guaranteed they would be delivered to Mears in person on his arrival in the capital.

Gratified by this outpouring of generosity and good will, Mears thanked everyone for the special gifts and for the friendships he and Jane had enjoyed with the people of Anchorage. Then, with a wry grin, he told the gathering that when the swords were "not being used," they would always remind him of the years he had been privileged to work in Alaska.

Clearly in high spirits, Mears briefly summarized the project, stressing the importance of the railroad as a means of developing the country. He challenged the government to support its completion as quickly as possible. Then he gave assurances that work on the Anchorage harbor would continue in his absence and that another construction season would finish the line to Seward, leaving only a small gap in the system north to Fairbanks.

Mears further promised that, upon his arrival in the capital, he would immediately take steps to avert possible strikes among the AEC's coal miners. To cover the differential cost of living between Alaska and the States, he said, he would propose the adoption of an equitable wage scale for the miners. Commissioner Edes led the rousing cheers that followed. Although a sense of sadness prevailed, the dancing soon began, and the festivities ended memorably.

The next morning, like all January mornings in the far north, was cold and dark. The somber reality of the Mearses' departure was relieved by a sprinkling of light snow. A crowd of well-wishers braved the weather to be at the station. Mears, in warm military attire, and Jane, in a long, black wool coat with a matching fur hat and muff, were prepared for the elements. The Mearses never sought public approbation for work they undertook—it was not in their nature. Nevertheless, as the train for Seward pulled away from the depot, the couple stepped out onto the observation deck to wave one last goodbye. The townspeople returned the gesture until the train was out of sight.

The townspeople bid farewell to Major Mears and his family as he leaves for duty in World War I France.

Familiar with the wiles of the weather along Turnagain Arm, Mears had allowed extra time to cope with the snow slides that sometimes covered the track during January thaws. Should an avalanche occur, passengers would have to portage their belongings over the frozen barricades to catch a waiting train on the other side. Fortunately, the Mearses were spared that inconvenience and needed only to climb onto bobsleds that stood ready to carry them between the unfinished portions of the line. The family would wait in Seward until time to board the steamship *Alaska* for Seattle.

The newest editor of the *Seward Gateway*, Elmer Friend, took Mears' appearance in town as an opportunity to waylay the commissioner one more time. When the two men met at the local hotel, Mears seemed more interested in enjoying his children than speculating about railroad matters, which he felt he'd left in capable hands.

Commenting on the acerbic article Friend published about the fruitless interview, Christensen wrote to Edes:

> You would think that when a man gives up the lucrative position that Major Mears had to go to the front, and sacrifices not only the position he held but possibly his life, in the interest of the nation, they would at least let him alone, instead of slurring him in this manner.

Realizing there was no use in trying to bring the towns together until the railroad was connected to Seward, Christensen determined that the only course for the commission was to proceed in any way that would best assure the success of the railroad project as a whole, "without regard to whether it benefits or hurts any particular section or town."

Little did anyone know that in less than two years' time, Mears would be back on the job to make the final calculations and decisions for the completion of the railroad.

## RECRUITS STEP FORWARD

In Washington D.C. on January 25, 1918, Mears was commissioned colonel in the national army. He would serve as commanding officer of the 31st Railway Engineers under Brigadier General W. W. Atterbury, director general of the American military lines in France. Lane had asked Mears to come to his office at noon on the day following the promotion. As a surprise, the secretary had also invited a number of Mears' friends and associates to join them. Among those present were Edes, Riggs, and employees of the AEC's Washington office, together with officials from the General Land Office, the Geological Survey, and the Bureau of Mines.

After the guests greeted Mears, Secretary Lane presented him with the two beautiful sabers that had been photographed for the Anchorage celebration. Echoing Christensen's words, Lane expressed his appreciation for the service Mears had rendered so well in Alaska on behalf of the government. In his farewell to Mears, he said,

> I wish you to know that the Interior Department is proud of you. You have left friends behind, friends who believe in you as one who has gone into this great adventure with a stout heart and a splendid willingness to sacrifice. We have your name on a roll of honor at the main entrance of our new building, but this is only a symbol of the respect we have for you. . . .

On departing for Fort Leavenworth, Kansas, where the 31st Regiment would be mobilized, Mears left notice of his resignation from the AEC, effective at the close of business on January 31. By the first of March, he and a team of assistants were actively canvassing the western states for experienced railroad men. In addition to the large contingent from Alaska, others were recruited from Seattle, Portland, Salt Lake City, San Francisco, Denver, and other western cities. Many beyond draft age volunteered their services. Still more were chosen from the 318th Engineers stationed at Vancouver Barracks, Mears' father's old post, and from Camp Dodge, Iowa, where Ned now held the rank of colonel and served as finance officer of the 88th Division. The two brothers worked together selecting personnel from that division.

In all, nine railroad regiments, each composed of thirty-three officers and approximately one thousand men, would be sent overseas after having first received a complete orientation at Fort Leavenworth. Most of the men had very little or no military experience, but they cooperated in the training exercises even though they were unlikely to be called for combat duty. Their job was to build and operate railroads.

The Mears family on the grounds of Fort Leavenworth, Kansas, 1918. Left to right, Jo, Jane, Helen, Betty, Colonel Mears, Freddy.

Throughout the recruitment and training period, Jane and the children had been staying with Mears at Fort Leavenworth. When the time came for him to leave, he put them on a train for Chicago, where they would live with her mother, Josephine Wainwright, for the duration of the war. Having grown up as the daughter of a cavalry officer, Jane stoically accepted the demands of separation. Still, concerned for her husband's welfare, she placed a ring for safety on his hand as they bid each other goodbye.

General John J. Pershing, commander in chief of the American Expeditionary Forces, had concluded early on that the success of the AEF during the critical summer and fall of 1918 hinged not upon ships but upon rail transportation. The narrow-gauge French railroads were too few in number to relieve the roads clogged with trucks, ambulances, and horse-drawn equipment carrying supplies and men to the front and casualties to the rear. The arrival of American troops seriously overburdened their system. Pershing saw that what the army needed was a solid railroad that could be thrown back together in a few hours after a big shell had demolished a few rods of it. This meant that the Americans' first line of duty upon landing would be to create, equip, and operate a standard-gauge railroad equal to that task.

At the general's direction, one massive convoy after another sailed from American ports, loaded with railroad building materials and lumber for the construction of roundhouses, coaling stations, repair shops, storage, and camps for the men. One shipment alone included thirty-six eighty-ton locomotives. The work of Mears' 31st Railway Engineers would be pivotal in reassembling those materials for actual use in France.

The operating battalion of Mears' regiment traveled in three sections by train and ferry to Hoboken, New Jersey, their port of embarkation. Then, on June 7, the men boarded the S.S. *Manchuria*, one of six naval transports in the convoy. As the vessel sailed out of New York harbor, past the Statue of Liberty, everyone sang, "Keep the Home Fires Burning." The voyage lasted twelve days.

## BEHIND FRONT LINES

Because all entry points on the English Channel were overloaded, destroyers escorted American ships to ports on the Atlantic coast of France. Among these was St. Nazaire, which handled over a third of all the supplies for the areas where the 31st was to operate. On the morning the *Manchuria* docked at St. Nazaire, Mears could see that his regiment had arrived none too soon. A vast jumble of supplies lay scattered about on the wharves. On disembarking, the colonel put his men directly to work organizing the confusion.

One week later, the regiment left St. Nazaire by train to Tours, 3.5 miles east of Saumur. This quaint town on the banks of the Loire River, was home to some 18,000 inhabitants when Colonel Mears and his engineers arrived. The 31st would set up Camp Strathcona near there.

The first night, the regiment slept in pup tents on what had previously been a plowed potato field and vineyard. The next day, all available men were detailed to reconstruct a number of abandoned barracks on the site into habitable quarters. Some were put to work constructing furniture for the mess halls, additional barracks, sanitation facilities, and double-tier bunks to accommodate four men each. Sixty-eight men were able to complete one barracks building in less than nine hours, and most of the work was completed in about two months. By then, the men were eager to get down to active railroading. After a short course in infantry drill, they were gradually absorbed into the primary job at hand.

The operating battalion was made up of ninety-three engineers, seventy conductors, fifty-five flagmen, ninety-three firemen, twelve trainmen, seven yardmasters, fifteen switch tenders, two roundhouse foremen, and twenty laborers. Others served as dispatchers, inspectors, machinists, boilermakers, plumbers, blacksmiths, electricians, carpenters, car-inspectors, riveters, police, cooks, and helpers.

*Mears collection*

In France during WWI, Colonel Mears (fourth from right) commanded the 31st Railway Engineers and later served as general manager of American army trains for the Transportation Corps.

By autumn of 1918, Mears' 31st Engineers had installed hundreds of miles of railroad track and reassembled a large number of locomotives and machinery. In addition, they had overseen the construction of 3.6 million square feet of covered storage and about 6 million square feet of open storage to house vast quantities of food, clothing, and military equipment, plus sufficient cold storage for more than 30,000 sides of beef.

One major accomplishment of the engineers was to replace the single-track railroad operated by the French with a double-track system. Thus, the French procedure of dispatching trains at half-hour intervals gave way to faster service, allowing up to five times that frequency. Without the backing of an uninterrupted transportation system, neither the stevedores at the seaports nor the riflemen on the front could function, and the work of the sailors on the freighters and the factory hands across the Atlantic would have lost its effectiveness.

Mears had everything he needed in France to carry out the work he was detailed to do. Unlike the project in Alaska, this one did not require long waits for federal appropriations, and Mears was free to address the needs that confronted him on a daily basis. Impressed by Mears' managerial and executive abilities, General Atterbury moved him from Camp Strathcona to Tours to serve as assistant general manager of railroads for the Transportation Corps, which by then numbered 50,000 troops. There, Mears befriended the local people, offering them the help of his men in repairing roads and digging wells for fresh drinking water.

Before long, Atterbury again promoted Mears to general manager of the American army trains. In that capacity, Mears was expected to keep in constant contact with all trains leaving base ports by means of a telegraphic numbering system monitored from the railroad record office at Tours. In addition, he made regular inspection tours of the divisions within the Transportation Corps at Angers, Saumur, Nantes, La Rochelle, Thouars, Le Mans, and other towns. Occasionally he used the general's open motor car on these missions. On one such trip, Mears sustained a blow to his head when a shell detonated near his moving vehicle. Fortunately, only his metal helmet was grazed in the incident, and he continued in his role as general manager until May 1919.


## LANE APPLIES PRESSURE

In Mears' absence, Lane became increasingly dissatisfied with the work in Alaska. He had hoped to have the railroad in complete operation by the end of the war, but that would not occur. Decidedly at a disadvantage without the original commissioners, he knew he needed Mears to pull the project together. Early in 1919, he wrote the secretary of war explaining his dilemma and asked that Colonel Mears be relieved from his duties in France and reassigned to his former work in Alaska. By that time, the armistice had been signed, and Atterbury was willing to release him. With the general's consent, then, the wheels were set in motion for Mears to return to the United States.

Before leaving France, Mears received the Grand Cross of the French Legion of Honor, personally conferred upon him by Maréchal Henri Pétain, commander in chief of the French army. Regarded as one of the ablest officers in the Transportation Corps, he also won the Distinguished Service Medal. General Pershing himself presented the award. Patting Mears on the back he said, "Atta boy, now go and build us a railroad."

Mears may have been reluctant to leave. He had found much satisfaction and challenge in the work he'd been given in France. And, at this juncture in his life, he could have exercised his option of retiring from military service to take work in the private sector at higher pay than the government could offer. The opportunity to return to Alaska, however, overshadowed these considerations and even began to dispel any lingering disappointment he felt at not having been able to complete the railroad there. Upon receiving his army orders to proceed to the U.S., he saluted farewell to Europe and braced himself for the work ahead on home soil.

*Mears collection*

Colonel Frederick Mears received the Grand Cross of the French Legion of
Honor from Maréchal Henri Pétain at the close of WWI.

**CHAPTER 11**

# ENTRUSTED WITH FULL COMMAND

*Commissioner Mears is on the job again . . . at home so to speak. . . .Things don't seem natural unless the quiet, unassuming commissioner is about.*

*Anchorage Daily Times*
September 1919

When Mears broke the news to the family that Secretary Lane had asked him to return to Alaska, they were overjoyed. Jane knew how much her husband had wanted to complete the railroad. This was his chance. Now, in high spirits, she and the older girls immediately began preparing for their trip to New York to meet the colonel on his return from Europe.

In May 1919, the transport carrying Mears and hundreds of other officers and soldiers—many of them bandaged or on crutches—steamed slowly into New York harbor. With the war over, vessels crowding the waterway displayed flags of all nations to welcome the ships returning home. Whistles blew and small brass bands played familiar war tunes, as the noisy crowd on the wharf strained to catch sight of loved ones. When the gangplanks lowered, cheering and shouting rose to a fever pitch, and the soldiers began to disembark. Spotting his own family, Mears rushed to embrace them. Baby Helen was already two years old, and talkative little Freddy easily gained his father's attention. By this time, Jo and Betty were almost teenagers, characteristically playful one moment and overly serious the next.

The family traveled by train to the capital and settled once again in their familiar Q Street quarters. Then, in keeping with army orders, Mears reported in person to the War Department to register the exact date and time of his return to the U. S. Next, in accordance with his agreement with Lane, he went directly to the AEC offices in the Department of Interior. There he met Lane's bright young assistant, John W. Hallowell, whose straightforward manner and attentiveness to detail were qualities Mears could appreciate. William Edes was also present. His health had failed considerably, but Lane was retaining him because of his first-hand knowledge of the railroad's construction activities.

After an initial round of greetings, Hallowell pulled up a chair for Mears at a large conference table nearby. Here, for the next three months, the group would hold meetings with professional geologists and railroad engineers in preparation for a full-blown inspection of the railroad later in the summer. The team would then return to the capital to consolidate a report of their findings, in justification for the AEC's $17 million funding request to continue the work.

## ARMED FOR ACTION

Mears found he clearly had some catching up to do. For several days he pored over photos, topographical information, correspondence, and reports that had passed between Lane, Edes, and those in the territory left in charge of the work. It was heartening for him to see recent photos of the S.S. *Admiral Watson*, secured to Gerig's dock at Ship Creek discharging passengers and freight, and of Edes driving the last spike that finally closed the gap between Seward and Anchorage in September 1918.

He was equally impressed with the extent of other work that had been accomplished in his absence. One hundred sixty-eight miles of new main line were in operation, and wagon roads had been built to get supplies and outfits into camps. Anchorage now had a safe supply of water, since the AEC had installed water tanks, pumping stations, water mains and sewers. In addition, the AEC's purchase and upgrading of the narrow-gauge Tanana Valley Railroad out of Fairbanks for $3 million, not only had given the commission access to the subbituminous coal near Nenana but also had rescued Fairbanks from a serious fuel famine.

Riggs had resigned from the AEC in April 1918, to serve as Governor of Alaska. He remained in an advisory capacity to the commission for another six months. Frederick D. Browne was transferred north to carry out the work Riggs had begun. A locating engineer formerly with the Southern Pacific Railroad, Browne had assisted Mears earlier in establishing the route from Matanuska Junction to Montana Creek on the Susitna River.

The state of the art at the time, in terms of railroad construction in Alaska, did not meet every need, as Browne was to discover. Conditioning the Tanana Valley Railroad was a major assignment in itself, but trying to extend the line farther south through the meandering river country proved to be a disaster. During the winter of 1918-19, out of concern over inadequate fuel supplies for Fairbanks residents, Browne threw his engineer's care to the wind and worked his crews overtime to lay track and trestles on the frozen muck and bogs to reach Burns Coal Mine south of Nenana before April. He made it in time to ship the coal north, but none too soon. Shortly after completion of the mission, an unforgiving spring run-off arrived with a raging torrent of water that washed away practically all evidence of Browne's labor.

After reviewing the report of this unfortunate episode, Mears girded himself for the censure that he knew would follow. He also determined that, regardless of how long it would take to complete the railroad, speed would have to be sacrificed for safety.

At the national level the advisability of the railroad project remained under scrutiny. The fact that the government had received repeated complaints about its coal mining operations in Alaska, which threatened to compete with commercial development, no doubt was cause for concern. But there had been no other choice. The government needed to open a mine in order to obtain coal for the engines on its railroad. In fact, part of the $2 million emergency appropriation by Congress had been specifically allocated for those purposes.

Toward the end of the war, Alaska's outspoken delegate, James Wickersham, led the quest to do something about the issue. In this case, he was not opposed to coal mining by the commission or by the navy for their stated purposes. Rather, he thought it was time Congress took action to give Alaskans release from the oppressive control the syndicate had over extraction of coal in Alaska and its shipment out of the territory. What Wickersham wanted was to have Alaska's coal leasing law placed upon the same footing as in the States, providing operators in the field with the same choice of lease and purchase that was granted elsewhere. Lane supported the concept, while admitting Alaska's coal leasing law had been a rank failure.

Most congressmen were in accord with Wickersham on this matter. Some were annoyed that certain individuals had become inordinately wealthy just by virtue of finding something valuable in the ground, when a large share of finding it had been done through the U. S. Geological Survey. Indeed, throughout Mears' tenure in

Alaska, he was often at the syndicate's mercy and hard-pressed to secure reduced shipping rates from them. On top of this they were not always reliable, more interested in handling their own business before processing the AEC's freight.

In the face of these difficulties, Mears prepared to return to Alaska, knowing full well he would have to wait for his appropriations and continue to deflect the ongoing criticism of the AEC's work. An open letter to Alaskans spelling out the complaints was among the papers he found on his desk. The *Anchorage Daily Times* printed the piece in its entirety in April 1919, and severely chastised its author, "a fellow named Drayton—Thomas B. Drayton, to be more polite. . . . Politeness costs nothing, otherwise we should not employ it when dealing with the person under discussion."

Secluded in the town of Seward, Drayton, all by himself, had established a phantom organization called "The Alaska Association," serving as its president, secretary, and treasurer. The *Times* described the effort as "ill-begotten, ill-conceived and ill-omened" and poked fun at the man's attempts to solicit money from "all true Alaskans." According to the Drayton letter, the purpose of the association was twofold:

> To houseclean and simultaneously effect an immediate prosecution of the project—under the pseudo-management of Mr. William C. Edes and those in charge under his alleged direction. Much can yet be salvaged by practical and competent railroad builders.

Drayton's anonymous source, the *Times* speculated, was "without a doubt . . . none other than John Ballaine."

On reading these remarks, Mears recognized that completing the railroad was going to call for a strenuous effort on all fronts, political and otherwise. He must have wondered what sort of a welcome he and his traveling companions would receive once they arrived in Seward.

## UNDER INSPECTION

One of the last orders of business transacted before the investigatory team left for Alaska took place shortly after Edes officially resigned from the AEC. At that time, Secretary Lane appointed Mears to serve as both chairman and chief engineer of the commission. The designated salary would remain "ten thousand dollars per annum less his pay as an officer of the Regular Army," essentially the same terms as his first appointment.

Those chosen to travel north were experienced railroad engineers and men familiar with the territory. They came with goodwill toward the project and were eager to see it completed. After thoroughly canvassing the railroad, they were to return with constructive advice regarding its operation and recommendations for its improvement. Lane appointed Hallowell as his personal representative to head the group.

Prominent on the list of those who accompanied Hallowell aboard the Alaska steamship liner *Alameda,* was renowned geologist Alfred Hulse Brooks, chief of the U.S. Geological Survey/Alaska Branch, making his twenty-first trip to Alaska. Others in the group were Colonel George T. Slade, former vice-president of the Northern Pacific Railway; S. M. Felton, president of the Chicago Great Western Railway; and Ralph Budd, vice-president of the Great Northern Railway. All were friends and former associates of Mears. Also on board were the entire Mears family and Mrs. Hallowell. Governor and Mrs. Thomas Riggs were to join the group at Juneau. The trip would require a month's time.

It was almost two years since Mears had left Alaska. The familiar shorelines, shrouded in mist, evoked memories of those first breathtaking encounters he'd had with the north land in 1914. And, much to his relief, when the huge steamer approached the dock in Seward, the naysayers were absent. Instead, crowds of exuberant citizens and railroad personnel were on hand to welcome the delegation to their town. William Gerig, along with other

*Mears collection*

Colonel Mears and Jane with young Freddy aboard the S. S. *Alameda*, returning to Alaska, August 1919.

railroad officials and friends of Edes and Mears, had traveled by train from Anchorage to greet the party as well.

The next day everyone was up early, ready to learn more about the town of Seward and to inspect the facilities of the Alaska Northern Railroad, now property of the U. S. government. At noon, everyone boarded the upgraded train for Anchorage to find comforts and amenities they hadn't expected. Lunch was served in the dining car, replete with white tablecloths and spotless tableware.

William Gerig and Colonel Mears enjoying the train
ride from Seward to Anchorage, August, 1919.

Mears had taken this part of the train trip many times before,
but this was his first uninterrupted ride around the circuitous loops
and through the tunnels in the mountainous Kenai country connecting Seward with Turnagain Arm. Traveling along the Turnagain
waterway on roadbed that had been blasted from the base of the
mountains, Mears could recount for his guests many of the construction dramas that had taken place there. Now, another thicket
of obstacles lay ahead to the north where the major bridges had yet
to be built. These thoughts brought with them a renewed sense of
urgency to return to work.

Hours later, in the lingering northern sunlight, the train pulled into the Anchorage station. Jubilant, flag-waving townspeople met the contingent. Members of the railroad staff were also there, as well as personal friends of the Mearses bearing bouquets of wildflowers. On catching sight of their house, the children raced to see who could get there first. The place was in Bristol condition, ready to welcome the family and the Hallowells, who were to be their guests.

The next morning, Mears and Gerig guided the officials on a close inspection of the AEC's port facilities and railroad terminal. Later, in the commission's offices, they reviewed contour maps indicating the route chosen for the railroad between Anchorage and Fairbanks. That evening, a public reception and dinner for the dignitaries took place in the Anchorage Chamber of Commerce room of the Empress Theatre building. Optimism prevailed as the group

*Mears collection*
William Gerig, second from left, Colonel Mears, and Governor Thomas Riggs celebrating the new Anchorage dock, 1919.

*AEC G-1422 Anchorage Museum of History and Art*
The new dock under construction at Anchorage.

enthusiastically discussed the future of Anchorage and the country contiguous to it. Mears was pleased to observe how attentively everyone studied the large black-and-white panoramic photograph of the harbor improvements and new dock displayed across one wall of the room. The scene depicted a dream come true and positive proof of the area's expansion capabilities.

The following day, the entourage rode the railroad's branch line through stretches of agricultural and grazing land in the Matanuska Valley where a few hardy pioneers had established homesteads. Continuing on, they stopped for a closer view of the coal seams protruding from the hillsides for miles. Looking up at the massive outcrops, the visitors generally felt that there must be enough coal in sight to heat America for the next hundred years.

Brooks agreed. He told them that steaming tests of the bituminous coal there had proved it to be equal to the best coal shipped from the east. Although those coal seams were bent and broken in comparison to the continuous horizontal beds in the east, everyone could understand why coal shipped directly from Alaska for the navy's Pacific fleet would be more economical than paying the exorbitant costs of transporting it across the country. Then, too, the opening of additional mines along the railbelt would bode well for the government's investment.

The tour would have been incomplete without the visitors' having an opportunity to actually experience the land Mears had grown to know so well. He assembled everything they would need for an outing: camping gear, pack horses, mosquito netting, and rough-weather clothing for all. The entire party, including women and children, rode the rails northward to the end of the line at mile 227. There they offloaded the gear and set out to enjoy the wilderness for a few days.

*Mears collection*

The Hallowell team visits a coal mine at Matanuska. Mears, far left; Alfred Brooks, left; Mrs. Hallowell, center; Riggs, right; John Hallowell, far right.

*Mears collection*

Jane enjoyed accompanying her husband on wilderness outings and held her own in marksmanship.

*Mear collection*

The Mears family enjoyed sharing the Alaskan wilderness with visitors, often taking their guests hunting and fishing.

At ease in the out-of-doors, Mears was in his element as he led the visitors up into the open country of Broad Pass. They all had an opportunity to hunt for caribou and sheep, to shoot duck, ptarmigan, or geese, and to catch fish. In the evening, they pitched tents and cooked meals over an open fire and traded jokes about the misadventures of cheechakos. At the end of the expedition, Slade, Budd, and Felton assembled their trophies and joined Mrs. Hallowell, Jane, and the children on their return trip by train to Anchorage. For those who had never been to Alaska, it was the experience of a lifetime.

Separating themselves from the others, Brooks, Hallowell, and Mears rode their horses over the graded right-of-way between mile 227 and mile 265, and along the trail marking the right-of-way to Nenana. Riggs had established the northern headquarters for the railroad there at the confluence of the Nenana and Tanana rivers.

*Mears collection*

Left to right: Alfred Hulse Brooks, Assistant U.S. Secretary of Interior John W. Hallowell, and Colonel Mears, inspecting the work in Alaska.

The largest tributary of the Yukon River, the Tanana was used in the early 1900s as a main artery for travel and freight. Now, the addition of train service would greatly expand transportation into the interior.

The railroad was to cross the Tanana at the town of Nenana, en route to the northern terminus at Fairbanks. Selection of a favorable bridge site, however, was proving to be no small challenge. Passing through the Nenana River canyon, the three men gathered soil samples and took pictures of the devastation that had destroyed Browne's bridge the previous spring.

At this point, Mears bid farewell to his companions and, alone on horseback, made a careful inspection of the right-of-way work that had been completed during the past summer at Carlo Creek, 136 miles south of Fairbanks. The other two men continued on to Fairbanks and then over the Fairbanks-Chitna trail to Cordova before returning to the States by steamer. By the end of the journey, Hallowell concluded that only Providence knew as much about Alaska as Alfred Brooks.

At home in Anchorage, Jane received a welcome message from the Hallowells thanking her for the hospitality she and her husband had shown them while in Anchorage. In a post script to the message, Hallowell added that Secretary Lane had every confidence Colonel Mears would succeed in completing the project with his forces well organized for the busy times ahead.

## LANE'S LAST WISH

Meanwhile, Lane was diligently preparing his annual AEC report for President Wilson. In the document he explained that the railroad was more than two-thirds built. "Congress," he wrote, "was impressed with the work of the Hallowell delegation and the showing it made that the road was built entirely without graft or touch of politics." Further, he could report that after "exhaustively examining into the work," the legislative body had authorized the AEC's $17 million funding request. Of those funds, $6 million was to be released immediately, $7 million in June 1920, and the $4 million balance in March 1921.

Although several bills had been introduced on the subject, Lane's grand plans for an Alaska development board never materialized. The idea had fallen apart after Alfred Brooks questioned the risks involved. In concept, Brooks approved the consolidation of land and soil activity in Alaska, but he feared his ongoing efforts could be lost or cut off altogether by new administrators wanting to bring their own specialists into the management arena. Finally, the notion was shelved because it would be years before the suggested governing board could gain the experience to match that of the bureaus. Even Lane realized they were getting nowhere.

By November 1919, Secretary Lane wanted to resign. He was ready to accept an offer he'd received for a more lucrative position outside of government, but he did not want to cause any embarrassment or added burden for President Wilson who was now ill. He waited until February 1920 to notify Wilson of his intentions. Even then, he was still dreaming of possibilities for Alaska. To his mind, creating traffic for the railroad was critical to progress there. Beyond promoting resource development, he wanted to see roads built to connect the mining settlements with the railroad and to initiate opportunities for livestock industries and farming. Confident in the AEC's abilities, he further believed the commission's powers should be expanded to oversee all of those endeavors. But his reach exceeded his grasp.

When Franklin Lane died a year later, in May 1921, Mears lost a friend and confidant. Although they did not agree on everything that took place during the construction of the railroad, Mears respected the man for his willingness to seriously consider both sides of problems that affected the northern work before handing down decisions.

Lane's resignation forced a considerable change in the administration of the railroad. John Barton Payne, a highly regarded lawyer and jurist from Chicago, would succeed him as Secretary of Interior in April 1920. Alexander T. Vogelsang was to serve as acting secretary for the interim. At this juncture, Frederick Mears was left on his own to serve as the embodiment of the Alaska Engineering Commission. Secretary Lane had placed all of the remaining work of the railroad under Mears' sole surveillance.

**CHAPTER 12**

# EQUAL T0 THE TASK

*The people here extend to Commissioner Mears their
sympathies in the problems he is up against. We are
with him to the finish.*

Fairbanks News-Miner
December 1920

Fighting the Great War had depleted supplies and manpower
for the AEC no less than it had drained the nation of resources. By
the time Mears returned to Alaska, the available work force had
dwindled to nearly 2,550, though some of the most challenging
work lay ahead. The railroad had yet to cross the largest rivers and
bridge the great divides separating important destinations on the
line. All the same, insistent pressure continued to emanate from
Washington to get on with the job and finish it soon.

While Mears was overseas, the interior secretary and Charles Curry, chairman of the House Committee on Territories, had been subjected to a relentless barrage of critical distortions about the management of the railroad. The instigator behind the fracas was Mears' old antagonist, John Ballaine. Using his sure-fire powers of persuasion, he not only had managed to induce a number of publishers to print and distribute his "newsworthy concerns" but also had succeeded in gaining an interview to discuss them with Lane.

During their meeting, as Ballaine expounded upon his doubts about the effectiveness of the AEC, Lane saw immediately that what the man really wanted was a job. Ballaine went so far as to suggest that he should be allowed to take over the management and entire operation of the line. He believed he was more than qualified for the work because of the extent of his railroad experience in Alaska. Lane had sympathy for him, but, at the same time, he knew Ballaine should have cut his losses long ago and moved on.

Another skeptic about the railroad's activities throughout this period was Alaska's respected delegate James Wickersham, author of the Alaska railroad bill. Before his election to Congress in 1908, he had served as judge of the third judicial district of Alaska, which extended from Valdez to Rampart, from Rampart to Circle, and from Circle to Eagle on the Yukon River. Having made himself popular with many of the sourdoughs in the region by rendering bold and impartial decisions on their behalf, he was not without friends.

Wickersham was a proud, somewhat testy man who demanded respect. Still smarting from the Guggenheims' rejection of his application to be their legal counsel years before, he took advantage of his congressional position to expose the dictatorial dealings of the Guggenheims in Alaska. Further rebuffed by Wilson's appointment of Riggs to the AEC and by the president's lack of regard for the Alaskans he'd nominated, Wickersham relentlessly criticized the commission's work. At every opportunity, he pointed out its inefficiencies and shortcomings, declaring emphatically that the railroad was losing money and that what the government needed was a developer.

It was no doubt clear to Mears that the total effect of those complaints had prompted Lane to rally support for bringing him back to complete the railroad in Alaska. This also explained why the Hallowell investigation of the railroad had been necessary, not only to justify the AEC's $17 million request but also to address and evaluate the adverse publicity the commission had received. In the face of these outside pressures, Mears would need to economize whenever possible in all aspects of the remaining work but

*Mears collection*

Alaska Engineering Commission staff circa 1920.
Left to right: Colonel Mears, chairman and chief engineer; C. L. Mason, chief clerk; William Gerig, assistant chief engineer; H. P. Warren, chief of supply; F. Hansen, maintenance and construction engineer; Burton Barndollar, examiner of accounts.

never at the risk of rendering a below-standard project. He had always understood his job in Alaska was to engineer the construction of the railroad, not to mastermind a profit-making venture.

When Mears returned to Alaska after the war, a 122-mile gap still existed between Anchorage and Fairbanks. Since the railroad between Seward and Anchorage was now connected, he combined both areas into the newly designated southern division. He appointed William Gerig, who had managed the Anchorage work so well during his absence, to serve as administrator and engineer-in-charge. In addition, all heads of construction, maintenance, mechanical, mining, transportation, and communication were directed to report to Gerig. Mears also consolidated the Fairbanks and Nenana areas into the northern division and appointed Frederick Browne engineer-in-charge.

## TROUBLE OVER THE TANANA

In 1914, when President Wilson stated, "The key to unlocking Alaska is a system of railroads," he was right. However, the keys that actually opened the land were the enormous steel bridges and viaducts that had yet to be built in the fall of 1919. Plans for the installation of these structures between Anchorage and Fairbanks—especially those crossing the Susitna River, Riley Creek, Hurricane Gulch, and the Tanana River—had been brewing in Mears' mind for several months. When the time came for action, he was ready to proceed on multiple fronts simultaneously.

The first bridges constructed by the AEC had been built from heavy timbers milled by commission crews. They crossed the major creeks and spanned the Matanuska, Knik, Eagle, and Talkeetna rivers. The most labor-intensive crossing work in the project's early years was the reconditioning of the old Alaska Northern's famous "loop" trestle, which followed a circular shape and crossed the railroad under itself to overcome the steep grades within the Kenai

*BL 79-2-1607 Anchorage Museum of History and Art*

To overcome the steep grades of the Kenai mountains, builders of the Alaska Northern employed this circular design for the rail line north of Seward. One accomplishment of the AEC was to recondition the loops and render them safe for heavily loaded trains.

mountains. At one time John Ballaine had maintained that purchase of the Alaska Northern Railroad would result in cost savings to the government. Rebuilding the line, however, proved to be hazardous and anything but economical for the AEC. Even after the improvements, a train trip over the structure was a thrill not unlike riding a roller coaster. Oftentimes, the weight of the locomotive alone would cause the trestle to sag and sway. When the swaying became especially great, the train would jump track and have to be reset with crowbars. This section was finally rendered safe for travel in September 1918, and continued to carry passengers until 1951. By then, the Bartlett Glacier had receded, and an alternate, more stable route was built over ground that thirty years earlier had been covered with seventy-five to one hundred feet of ice.

In 1916, the AEC got its feet wet in river operations when it built docks and various terminal facilities on the Tanana. More recently, while Mears was away in France, some bridge work had been undertaken at the small town of Nenana under the direction of Edes and Browne. Before Mears went overseas, he and Edes had discussed building a long, low, 200-foot multi-span bridge to connect the town to the opposite bank of the Tanana River. Mears had never warmed to the plan, although the design would accommodate river steamers equipped with hinged smokestacks. That, in his opinion, was its only advantage, and he seriously questioned its long-term stability.

Nevertheless, for reasons he believed necessary, Browne had installed timber piling to support a structure there. The piling had to be driven deep into sand and gravel because bedrock lay far below the water. As it turned out, during the spring run-off thick ice wore away those underpinnings until the temporary structure finally broke apart.

*Mears collection*

Bridges built early in the project were made of timber, as was this temporary pile trestle at Nenana River crossing, mile 373.

In September 1919, when the Hallowell team was in Alaska to investigate the status of the overall project, they saw the remnants of Browne's failed efforts. It was obvious to the group that rebuilding a permanent crossing in that location was out of the question. In the meantime, Mears had revised his calculations in favor of a single span without river piers. His reconnaissance of the area had led him almost a mile upstream where the waterway narrowed and a high span from bank to bank could cross above the channel.

The fact that Browne's structure had come to naught and that another would have to take its place did not sit well with the Fairbanks and Nenana commercial clubs. Reflecting Wickersham's bias, many club members took it upon themselves in the spring of 1920 to urge Secretary Payne to expedite construction of a replacement bridge over the Tanana. Arguing purely in their own interest, they asked the secretary to immediately ship the proposed steel structure—the design of which had not been finalized—into Nenana via the Yukon River route from St. Michael on the coast.

When Mears learned of their contact with Payne, understandably he was irritated. He countered by sending a lengthy letter to the secretary, detailing why it would be premature for him to act upon the commercial clubs' advice. On his most recent return to Alaska, he had stopped in Chicago to consult with the foremost engineering firm of Modjeski and Angier. Wanting another opinion about the proposed Tanana River crossing, he had asked them to send one of their resident engineers to Nenana in April to thoroughly analyze the bridge site with him. In reporting this to Payne, Mears pointed out that, although War Department standards required a 55-foot clearance over high water, a minimum of forty-five feet would suffice in this case. During the four-month summer season, much money had been lost in navigating the shallow Tanana River channels above the town of Nenana. Acknowledging this, he wrote:

> In my mind, to require excessive clearance for
> navigating that part of the stream would be an un-

necessary provision. It is quite doubtful whether river boats of any size will ever pass beyond Nenana as soon as the government railroad is on a substantial operating basis between Nenana and Fairbanks. On a bridge of this nature, the bridge companies would require from four to five months in which to prepare their estimates of cost. It is desirable that we proceed to call for bids soon, as it is only by the most energetic work that the bridge can be made available before the railroad is completed between Seward and Nenana.

Because of the complexity of the venture, Angier, the principal in the Chicago engineering firm, made the trip himself in April 1920, to assess the situation and confer with Mears. He and his engineers then translated Mears' concept into a design for a 700-foot, simple truss span rising forty-seven feet above mean summer high water. More than two years would pass before all the bridge components arrived in Alaska for assembly. Delegate Wickersham and the rest would simply have to wait.

## PASSING MUSTER

Mears' far-flung responsibilities kept him in almost daily communication with his division heads, with stations along the line, and with the purchasing office in Seattle, which processed ocean freight shipments to Alaska. To entice workers back to the territory, he placed bold ads in the Seattle newspapers offering all-expense-paid trips to Alaska and work with wages starting at $5 per day. Bridge carpenters could earn $7.50 per day.

The response was gratifying. In May 1920, the S.S. *Cordova* departed Seattle with seventy-five new hires for the AEC aboard, many of them European immigrants. A few, however, were intent

Mears (left) and Gerig (right) pause to celebrate steel rail
reaching mile 263.8 at Gold Creek, September 16, 1920.

only on seeing Alaska at the commission's expense, with no plans
at all for doing actual work for the railroad. Learning that seven of
the men had jumped ship, Mears immediately cabled the marshal
in Valdez to "round up those men and make them reimburse the

*Mears collection*
A steel-laying gang hard at work at mile 429 in the northern region, September 1919.

commission or come to Seward to fulfill their contracts." The amount due from each was $29.25—just under a week's pay and hardly indicative of the ordeal the laborers would face.

Only a few weeks earlier, a different kind of complication had seized the colonel's attention. Between April and May 1920, a serious influenza epidemic had broken out near Nenana, crippling industry and closing business in Fairbanks. Whole families were stricken at the same time. Hundreds of railroad employees suffering from fever and muscular pain brought on by the virus were incapacitated for several weeks. Remembering John Stevens' efforts to eradicate yellow fever in Panama, Mears immediately took action to avert spread of the disease. Cooperating with the Red Cross, he used all of the AEC's available manpower and facilities to meet the needs of those who required hospital care and medical attention. Due to his quick response, lives were saved and the disease was brought under control, but the AEC was out of pocket for an extra $5,000. Nine months later, the commission was finally reimbursed in a deficiency bill acted upon in the House. The payment, however, could not reinstate the time lost.

Secretary Payne soon found it prudent to spearhead his own investigations of the AEC's activities. Some were conducted more openly than others. Within months of his appointment to the interior post, he traveled to Alaska—something his predecessor had never done. During the middle of July 1920, accompanied by Secretary of the Navy Josephus Daniels and a group of government officials, Payne made a detailed on-site inspection of the line. One reason for the trip was to determine if there were any proof to the recurring negative reports circulating in Washington about the project. In the end, Payne's investigations confirmed there was simply no evidence to validate the charges against the AEC. If colossal corruption and mismanagement existed, the report said, it must

*AEC G-1597 Anchorage Museum of History and Art*

Secretary of Interior John Barton Payne (wearing raincoat) boards the *Betty M.*, one of the AEC's river tunnel boats, along the Susitna River.

have been concealed with consummate skill.

Since Payne's appointment, Mears had corresponded with him regularly on every aspect of the AEC's work in Alaska. Upon seeing Mears in action, the secretary was greatly impressed with his managerial skills and surprised to discover how much was expected of the man. Before long, Payne was a strong supporter of Mears, an attitude the colonel definitely welcomed. Later that year, the secretary would back Mears' efforts to encourage Anchorage residents to assume control of their town themselves.

With the coming of another presidential election, Mears decided in the fall of 1920 that it was time to place his position with the army in its proper context. Having served the greater part of his career as an engineer, not as a cavalry officer, he asked to be transferred from the cavalry to the Army Corps of Engineers. The War Department approved the request, and on November 14, 1920, Mears received his appointment as lieutenant colonel in the Corps of Engineers. His brother-in-law Jonathan Wainwright was Acting Secretary of War at the time and signed the papers making the appointment official.

## ANCHORAGE INCORPORATES

Young Anchorage was beginning to become a prosperous little town. Grocery and dry goods stores, churches, hotels, lumber companies, meat markets, and barbershops lined the main street of the town. Fancy haberdasheries sold Australian Brand Kangaroo jackets, Mackinaw coats, knickers and knee-high leather boots. For the women, long woolen suits were on display next to winter coats with matching hats.

As a couple, the Mearses continued to participate in the life of the community. Jane's leadership skills seemed to parallel those of her husband. She attended the Episcopal church regularly and

*AEC G-750 Anchorage Museum of History and Art*
The changing face of Fourth Avenue, the main street of Anchorage.

prepared teas in honor of visitors to Anchorage. An effective activist, she resumed her work for the betterment of educational facilities and cultural improvements in Anchorage.

Of growing concern in 1920 was whether or not the citizens of Anchorage were ready to take full responsibility for the operation of their town. They had a good thing in federal paternalism—their living was economical, scandal-free and carefree—and they were reluctant to give up the AEC's management. However, the five-year time allowance for incorporation of their town was about over. Territorial law required a two-thirds vote of the residents. If the vote were to fail, Anchorage would fall into administrative limbo.

Mears knew it was urgent for the people to take action. Members of his board were also worried. In October of that year, the commission's chief accountant, Burton Barndollar, a plainspoken individual who understood the seriousness of the situation, addressed a gathering of local citizens. He warned that the government had ended its period of control and that in the future it would have no more to do with the management of the town than it had with the management of Seattle. He urged that Anchorage not risk losing its opportunity for self-government. Failure to seize it, he said, would suggest to Washington that Alaska was populated by political hypocrites.

Alarmed by their predicament, those in attendance immediately nominated a slate of candidates for council seats and held an election concurrently with the balloting for incorporation. Unfortunately, after the election, the district judge in Seattle ruled the incorporation defeated. The townspeople were dismayed. "What went wrong? How could this be? What prompted it?" they asked.

Confounded by the outcome, Mears investigated the results himself and discovered that 85 blank ballots had been counted in opposition to incorporation. He fired off a telegram directly to the district attorney, urging him to file a brief against inclusion of the blanks. The district attorney agreed: the ballots should never have been counted in the first place because they carried no expression of opinion for or against. His argument was convincing enough to persuade the district judge to reverse his decision. Thus, on November 23, 1920, Anchorage was declared incorporated. The operation and management of the town was turned over to local authorities on December 1. At that time, the federal government relinquished control of the Anchorage townsite and granted patents to land sold five years earlier.

Mears was proud of the AEC's town-building efforts in Anchorage and along the railbelt. Although he knew the transition for the new town would be gradual, he was greatly relieved to know others would take over responsibility for it. At last he was free to give his full attention to the bridges, viaducts, and steel arches that would finally complete the magnificent transportation corridor across Alaska.

**CHAPTER 13**

# SPANS OF STEEL, WILL OF IRON

*It is a wild country through which the railroad is being constructed. If the people of the United States knew more about it, they would not stand aghast at the terrible expenditures.*

Edward E. Miller,
Illinois Congressman, 1921

When organizing the extensive excavation for the railbed in Alaska, Mears adopted the inventive plan Stevens had devised in Panama to use the railway power itself for removing hundreds of tons of spoil. To fully grasp the immensity of the task, Jack Lincke, a columnist for the *Anchorage Daily Times*, took the train from Anchorage to the end of steel in the middle of winter. There, he acknowledged seeing more activity and greater efficiency than he'd ever imagined:

> ... the construction of a trunk line carrying completion in every detail, even to permanent ballasting, in temperatures ranging from zero to 32 degrees below. And this being done with a smoothness equal to summer operation, without confusion and with only minor disruptions of a perfect schedule.

Lincke compared the scene to a battlefront with various bosses moving about the job like colonels, majors, captains, sergeants and corporals. Out there in "no man's land," he wrote, trains were de-

*Mears collection*

Looking south from mile 387.8, August 16, 1917

livering thousands of tons of railroad building materials including
narrow gauge dinkey engines. AEC "doughboys" unloaded the
freight onto big sleighs drawn by powerful Percheron teams of
four or six. Huge tractors would "snort, grumble and elbow" their
way through the snow, packing down roadbeds to the supply depots along the "firing line."

Those construction stations, ten miles apart, stood as emblems
of civilization dotting the wild country. Built mostly of log from
trees collected on site, they incorporated everything needed to get
the job done: bunkhouses for the laborers, a camp kitchen, storage
for food and supplies, and a stable for upwards of sixty horses.
Larger camps near the bridge construction sites included quarters
for supervisory staff and basic medical facilities. At night, the teamsters wrapped their faithful animals in blankets to guard them against
lung fever while cooling off and to ready them for the next morning's
big assignments.

*Mears collection*

Store at Residency 4, mile 373, August 25, 1917.

Mears' intent, Lincke reported, was for each of the stations to be made available to pioneers wanting to settle there, or to serve as operating bases for prospectors and tourists after the railroad work was finished. Although Mears was laying himself open to further criticism by establishing such well-equipped camps, he never considered providing his men with anything less.

## SUSITNA BRIDGE CHALLENGE

The lessons from the Tanana River experience caused Mears to rethink his ideas for a bridge across the Susitna River. In his early reviews of the 250-mile glacial waterway, 150 miles north of Anchorage, he had written, "It is necessary to stretch the imagination a little to say that the Susitna River is a navigable stream."

Therefore, before finalizing his plans for the approach spans leading to the bridge, he revisited the site once more during spring break-up. He was appalled to see the powerful waterway filled to overflowing with rocks, trees, and enormous shards of ice demolishing everything in their way. The high water marks along the shore and the ice scars on the trees he'd spotted when making his first calculations were no longer visible. Mears saw immediately that he would have to totally abandon his plan to support the structure on channel piers.

He needed no further information to convince his bridge engineers, W. E. H. Fogelstrom and F. H. Chapin, that the velocity of the water and ice would eliminate any consideration of supporting the bridge on timber or, for that matter, on concrete piers installed in the center of the river. Then, having ruled out those possibilities, Mears contracted with the American Bridge Company of Gary, Indiana, to revise the design and complete the manufacture of a steel span in time for winter erection.

The adopted location for the railroad closely followed the Susitna River. Marginal as this river might have been for navigation,

*AEC G-1769 Anchorage Museum of History and Art*
The 504-foot Susitna River bridge was completed in February 1921.

the AEC's small fleet of flat-bottomed barges had performed surprisingly well. Transportation difficulties eased off considerably when track was laid directly up to the bridge site itself. At the same time, in order to keep pace with the ongoing work, Mears directed crews to build a train trestle one hundred feet downstream, parallel to the centerline of the bridge. This temporary structure provided for the uninterrupted movement of railroad equipment to other construction sites farther north.

Because of the high price of steel and concrete, Mears used timber in building the long approach spans to the Susitna bridge. This was the kind of economy measure he had to employ in the construction of the entire line. Still, he readily admitted replacement with more permanent materials would be necessary at some later date.

Cement was reserved for building two immense concrete piers at opposite ends of the Susitna bridge, in October and December 1920. Mixing concrete during those months in temperatures dipping from zero to -42 degrees F. required skill. Everything, including the sand, gravel and water for the operation had to be heated. When the mixture was ready, it was poured through chutes into heavy canvas-lined, wooden-framed pier pits. For extra precaution, the piers were kept warm to ensure that the concrete would cure before coming into contact with the cold river water.

A partial failure of the first pier unfortunately occurred because the gravel contained humus. Undaunted, the builders located another source of gravel six miles distant. Then, after adding an extra percentage of sand to the mixture, they soon brought it up to standard. Over the years, the spring run-off may have eroded the exterior layer of concrete on those abutments but it has never carried them away.

The erection of the 1,803-ton steel superstructure was accomplished by American Bridge Company crews with the assistance of two large locomotive cranes. Of the thousands of field rivets that were driven on the bridge during the very cold weather, none were found to be faulty when retested several times in warmer temperatures.

The span for the Susitna bridge was swung on February 2, 1921, and the first train passed over it four days later. Engineers of the $900,000 crossing openly expressed their indebtedness to Mears for the explicit specifications he had given them for the project. At that time, the 504-foot structure was reputed to be the largest through truss single span west of the Mississippi River and the second largest bridge ever produced at the Gary, Indiana, plant.

Mears had no time to savor the fruits of his efforts because three more important crossings along the main line were also underway. The first lay twenty miles north of the Susitna bridge at Hurricane Gulch; the second, sixty-three miles beyond that at Riley Creek, just south of McKinley station. The third, an additional sixty-seven miles north, was at Nenana across the Tanana River. That project alone would be monumental for any engineer.

## BEST LAID PLANS

Not long after the partial collapse of the Susitna bridge pier, Mears was reminded once again that he was fighting more than forces of nature. Almost daily he was plagued with problems that had taken root while he was in France—problems that emanated from Delegate Wickersham and his loyal following in Fairbanks, and from John Ballaine in Seward.

Capitalizing upon the Susitna bridge pier failure, and surely with some encouragement from Wickersham, the Nenana Commercial Club, wrote again to Secretary Payne demanding that he fire commissioner Mears for incompetency. Club members estimated that completion of the railroad would be delayed for a year because of poor management. When the complaint was made public, it received widespread coverage in the press.

In December, the *Fairbanks News-Miner* wrote an open apology to Mears and to Governor Riggs, who had also come under fire by virtue of his former association with the commission. The editors had hoped the derogatory report would slip by and escape doing the community and Mears harm. It was one of those "gratuitous insults," they said, that great men have handed them occasionally. "When the railroad was voted for," they added, "nobody in Interior Alaska ever insinuated it would be passable before 1921. The people here realize while abuse of the builders might delay completion of the project, it cannot hasten it."

Soon, another letter found its way into the press—one written to Mears from E. M. Braford, construction foreman for the bridge. In defense of his company, Braford testified that the men who began work on the Susitna bridge in October were not delayed one day on account of the failure of the south pier. "Satisfactory arrangements were made," he wrote, "to enable them to continue their bridge building from the north end, which proved both convenient and economical to all concerned."

The failure of the pier would have passed unnoticed had it not been for the perseverance of Wickersham and Ballaine. They seemed to believe that by constantly badgering the builders and publicizing their shortcomings, they would wrest control of the project. Combined, their efforts created a strong adversarial force. Mears' only recourse in the face of those odds was either to acquiesce or to continue with the construction of the railroad on his own terms. He chose to stand his ground.

## HURRICANE GULCH, RILEY CREEK, AND "THROUGH SERVICE"

About two months before completion of the Susitna bridge, T. W. Secrest, AEC superintendent of construction, set up another log headquarters camp on the north bank of the Chulitna River at Hurricane Gulch in the heart of the Alaska Range. The large army of men working at this station were to lay track and construct bridges and trestles to reach the headwaters of the interior at Nenana. Watchmen on duty kept a vigilant eye on the camp and on the coal stoves that burned night and day. The doctor in charge maintained a fast horse in case of emergency.

Railroad crossings built over Hurricane Gulch and Riley Creek were trouble-free compared to the drawn-out drudgery of installing the Susitna River bridge. Construction rigors at the Hurricane site, however, were more demanding. From columnist Lincke's point of view, the scenic beauty of Broad Pass, rimmed by Mount McKinley, Mount Foraker, and hundreds of other peaks equaled the best scenery in the Canadian Rockies, Glacier Park and the high Sierras combined. But here at Hurricane Gulch nature had split open a level plateau with a deep gash 384 feet wide and nearly as far down into the bowels of the earth. "This," he wrote, "is the home of Boreas, the Storm King of Alaska, who when not sleeping, coughs chilling blasts down the gulch."

Confidence ran high during construction of the enormous hinged arch, buttressed as it was against solid rock on both sides.

*E. F. Bryant collection 72-129-19, Rasmuson Library, University of Alaska Fairbanks*
The Hurricane Gulch bridge under construction, 1921.

On-site photographs of the project at Hurricane defy belief. Crews, like trapeze artists suspended hundreds of feet in the air, rendered exacting performances as they moved about the unconnected scaffolding. Steam shovel operators, with their frosted mustaches and multiple layers of thick clothing, tirelessly dug excavations for the approach spans, leaving splotches of dirt on the carpet of snow in their wake. A four-ton cable way transferred unwieldy construction materials back and forth across the gulch, another adaptation of measures once used in Panama.

American Bridge Company crews began fabrication and cantilever erection of the 918-foot span on June 8, 1921. Sixty working days later, the first train passed over it. The bridge in its entirety, including the north and south approaches, is 1,322 feet in length. Fifteen-hundred tons of steel were used in its construction at a cost of $1.5 million.

A few hundred feet south of McKinley station, more workers were assisting in the erection of a structure across the Riley Creek gorge. Less dramatic than the Hurricane Gulch bridge, but still strik-

*BL 79-2-7643 Anchorage Museum of History and Art*
Construction camp at the Riley Creek bridge site.


ing, the Riley Creek span, supported by pyramids of steel, extends 500 feet over the creek. It was begun in December 1921 and completed in record time two months later.

By then, construction had progressed to the extent that the railroad offered "through service" over the 470-mile main line from Seward to Fairbanks. This train ride could have been promoted as the trip of a lifetime for those seeking adventure in the far north. But, as the commission had no extra time or funds for marketing, this service was offered only as a courtesy measure.

Those fortunate enough to be in Alaska, and hardy enough to take the trip in the home of the Storm King, discovered that "through service" meant they would cross unfinished gaps in the line on track temporarily installed over the icebound waterways of Riley Creek and the Nenana River canyon. Before the travelers reached their destination, another frigid adventure awaited them at

*William Wilson collection 84-16-19, Rasmuson Library, University of Alaska Fairbanks*
AEC river docks, Nenana, October 1920.

the town of Nenana. There, in temperatures from 25 to 45 degrees below zero, passengers were expected to transfer themselves and their luggage onto narrow-gauge railcars pulled by the North Nenana Limited, a "one lunger" dinkey engine used only during winter for hauling trains over the frozen Tanana. On the other side of the river, a locomotive from the old Tanana Valley Railroad was hitched on the run to carry passengers the rest of the way to Fairbanks.

This manner of transportation no doubt failed to measure up to the expectations of the Nenana Commercial Club. It was progress, however—visible progress. The commission's achievements in 1920 and 1921 were staggering. Colonel Mears' last major objective would be to bridge the Tanana River and thus provide the final link on the north-south route. He welcomed the challenge, rough as the going might be.

Locomotive crossing Ship Creek.

## CHAPTER 14

# A FIGHT TO THE FINISH

*The big, outstanding fact is that the Government has built a railroad in Alaska, penetrating a vast unknown wilderness, 5,000 miles distant from the federal seat, and with never a hint of graft or loot.*

Scott C. Bone,
Territorial Governor, 1922

Throughout this same period, counter to the exhilaration of completing the bridges, heated debate persisted over the escalating costs of the railroad and the effectiveness of its management. Consequently, the value of the project in general, and Mears' worth in particular, fell victim to attack from many sides.

With no real conception of the work ahead and impatient for immediate results, some legislators were reluctant to pour more and more money into the construction of a "railroad in the clouds." Others thought it would be better for the government "if the whole thing were scrapped!" All seemed to forget that their unwillingness to advance funds in a timely manner had been one of the major reasons for repeated delays.

When the AEC's $4 million appropriation bill came under consideration by Congress early in 1921, it had trouble passing. A large part of the problem lay in Secretary Payne's request that Colonel Mears' salary be increased from $10,000 to $15,000 per year. But Payne, having seen the extent of Mears' responsibilities as well as his capabilities in handling them, believed the increase was clearly justified, if not overdue. This request alone set off a political bomb-shell in the halls of Congress.

Representatives Martin B. Madden and William B. McKinley of Illinois, cohorts of Ballaine, took on the issue with a vengeance. In one outburst, Madden complained:

> Military men do not know money and do not
> care what is spent as long as it does not come out
> of their pockets. Someday I hope we will find some
> civilians who are qualified to act as commissioners
> to build the rest of the railroad and that when they
> are appointed they will go on the job and know
> how to conserve public money.

Not content to let it rest at that, Madden claimed the two civilian commissioners, Edes and Riggs, had never seen a railroad except when they rode on it. Both were paid $10,000 a year and, in his opinion, had done nothing for their compensation. Furthermore, he had seen no proof that coal had been found. In his doubt about the value of the whole project he added, "Sometimes they say if you want to get there you've got to dig through seventy feet of ice."

Another congressman from Illinois, Edward Miller, thought differently. A member of the House Committee on Territories, he held a more favorable view of the situation in Alaska. "Some people, from ignorance, are easily scandalized," he said. "I only wish that members of the House could see this railroad and the country through which it goes. . . .Alaska is the greatest asset held by any nation in the world, and I do want to see that road completed."

Anchorage columnist Jack Lincke, someone who had seen Mears in action, came to his defense by publishing his version of the full array of duties the commissioner was expected to carry out. He felt the man deserved to have something nice said about him for a change:

> If building railroads was all there was to the task of the Alaska Engineering Commission it would have been a sinecure for Colonel Mears. In addition to building the railway, Uncle Sam insisted that the work should be of a permanent nature, and on top of this he piled the onerous duties of creating, as he went, all the essentials of empire building— chief engineer, governor general, district committee man, dog catcher, ward heeler and town cop.
>
> In addition to being efficient, he must be a combination prize fighter, diplomat engineer, politician and social arbiter, with a hide as thick as a walrus and a poise that refuses to be tipped off its equilibrium by an Alaskan blizzard or one of the big shots set off by the powder gang.

The appropriation bill passed, but with a proviso inserted at the behest of Representative McKinley that "no individual shall be paid an annual salary out of this fund of more than $10,000." Mears would still receive the raise, however, because a portion of his pay would still be coming from the army. An April memo to Mears

from the AEC's examiner of accounts Burton Barndollar assured
him that his $15,000 salary for fiscal year 1922 would not be in
violation of McKinley's proviso because his officer's pay from the
Army Corps of Engineers would continue to be subtracted from
the amount he received from the AEC. Even at the higher rate, the
amount paid to Mears from the commission's funds would not exceed $10,000, so long as his army pay stayed at or above $5,000.
There seemed to be no further reason for concern about the matter, but that was a mistaken assumption.

## TEMPEST IN A TEAPOT

   With the change in administration from Woodrow Wilson to
Warren Harding as president, Washington politics were cast in a
different light. The attitude toward Alaska became skewed when
Harding appointed Albert Fall to replace John Payne as Secretary
of Interior. Fall's association with the president stemmed from his
tenure as senator from New Mexico—the two men had occupied
adjacent seats in the senate chambers. Now Fall would be responsible for all matters pertaining to Alaska, including the railroad.
   Harding told the nation he wanted to lead America into a new
era of prosperity. But his cabinet, and others who had orchestrated
his election, had their own agendas about how to usher in that era.
They were strong proponents of opening up the land and resources
of the nation for development by private interests. The underside
of their plans was based upon doling out contracts to wealthy entrepreneurs who stood ready to exploit those resources for their
own purposes.
   When Secretary Fall proclaimed that petroleum reserves should
never have existed in the first place, he became a prime suspect of
conservationists. Soon it was apparent that he and his friends were
after billions of dollars worth of natural resources held by the government. Within months of his appointment, he quietly leased na-

val oil field reserves in California and Wyoming. Investigations made the following year would reveal that the deals were made covertly with individual oil men and that Fall had received handsome pay-offs in return.

One of those reserves, a red sandstone formation rising dramatically out of the sagebrush flats of Wyoming, was thought to resemble a teapot. Known as Teapot Dome, it became the symbol of rampant corruption within the Harding administration. Ultimately, the scandal surrounding it would force Albert Fall to resign. In a case that remained unsettled until 1931, Fall was found guilty of conspiracy to defraud the government. This was the tenor of the times.

Evidence of how the tumult might affect Alaska surfaced shortly after Harding's election. Taking advantage of the manipulative character of the new president's cabinet, John Ballaine once again insinuated himself into the Washington scene. He attended hearings on appropriations for the railroad, gave lengthy, unsolicited testimony, and released highly embellished accounts of his activities. Through constant lobbying, he made contact with incoming Secretary Fall to present himself as someone who could do a better job than Mears as chairman of the AEC. Fall was so taken with Ballaine's persuasive arguments that he almost appointed him right then and there.

The implication of these endeavors was not overlooked. When a dispatch to the *Seattle Times* from a Washington correspondent reported that Fall was seriously considering Ballaine as a possible candidate to succeed Mears, it prompted a spontaneous flood of support for the colonel instead. Anticipating further delays and alarmed at the prospect of Ballaine at the helm, the Fairbanks Commercial Club immediately wrote Fall, asking him not to change the present personnel of the AEC. As tactfully as possible, they told him how Alaska suffered from the work of unauthorized persons who had taken it upon themselves to speak for the territory.

The Anchorage Chamber of Commerce followed suit in a cablegram to Fall, stating that Ballaine's constant harassment had

retarded the project at every step. They cautioned that to disrupt
the work now by replacing the head of the project so close to
completion, would be ill-advised and expensive. Territorial lawmakers as well wrote individually to the secretary, urging him to retain
the present management of the railroad and thereby enable the
territory to go forward in its development.

These insistent communications forced Fall to take another
look at Ballaine and to postpone making any changes in the management of the railroad. But Mears' political problems were far
from over. He would have to continue working with the new cabinet or walk away from the most important project of his career.
That he would not do.


## POSITIVE PUBLICITY

Possibly in an effort to surmount the uncertainty about the
AEC's efforts, Mears took to the road in February 1921, just after
completion of the Susitna bridge. By this time, he had become a
much sought-after public speaker. On what might be regarded as a
publicity tour, he presented a series of speeches on the status of
the railroad to a number of professional organizations and civic
groups in Seattle and Portland. Projecting six reels of his own
motion pictures, Mears invited his listeners to sit back and join him
on a trip aboard the government railroad into the wilds of Alaska.
He seemed to enjoy regaling his stateside audiences with stories of
the railroad workers and their accomplishments. Revealing his more
poetic side he was quoted as saying:

> Alaska, long the lure of gold seekers, where
> London found his graphic touch . . . is more than a
> land of hidden wealth and rugged ranges. . . . I will
> not paint an extravagant picture of Alaska, for I
> believe that by so doing more harm than good would

result. But that it is worth developing is beyond the shadow of a doubt. Alaska will repay America richly for the effort—but it holds forth no easy riches.

It had taken twenty-five to thirty years, he said, to develop the American West, which had been in immediate touch with other parts of the country. Endowed with immense land grants, railroad companies there had actively encouraged new settlements and the building up of traffic. To bring about similar results in a territory situated six or seven days' sailing time beyond the shores of the United States was significantly more difficult. In closing, he challenged everyone to consider the potential of Alaska, saying, "The future progress of the Territory will depend upon a permanent and stable system of industry that will operate only cheap and reliable methods of transportation."

## RATES LACED WITH CRITICISM

The commission had always been handicapped in the assignment of rates. Unlike the Panama Canal, where heavy commerce and naval traffic were virtually certain, the Alaska project began without promise of return. The mission of the AEC, after all, was construction, not operation. The chairman and chief engineer had authority to regulate freight rates within Alaska, but had no authority to establish overseas rate policy. That power resided with the Interstate Commerce Commission and the secretary of interior. However, as Mears represented the government in Alaska, it was he who worked with the steamship lines. The issue was complex. Some large and bulky items were not heavy, others were lightweight and fragile, and still others (like coal) required no special handling but were very heavy. Rates based on weight were fair in some cases, but the measurement basis made sense just as often. There was no easy answer.

All the while, Mears was subjected to conflicting messages about how to reckon with the problem. Skeptics in Washington criticized him for not making a profit. Wickersham and others complained that the AEC's rates were so high they were stifling development in the territory. Urging a rate reduction, George Preston, an agent for the Northern Commercial Company in Fairbanks, counseled Mears:

> It was not intended or expected that the railroad would accumulate profits or even pay operating expenses at the start, but that it should be administered more in the nature of a public service, somewhat analogous to the postal service— to facilitate the opening up of rich new territory which, owing to unusual conditions, could not be developed . . . by private enterprise alone.

Trotting out his old vendetta against the Guggenheims, Ballaine had charged in 1919 that the AEC was allowing them to dictate its policies, resulting in exorbitant rates. To this Edes had countered,

> In justice to the Alaska Syndicate, I will say I know of no attempt on their part to influence our policy or block our progress. It is true that we have reluctantly paid some pretty heavy freight rates but that experience has not been confined to Alaska.

By November 1921, with "through service" almost a reality, Mears appointed a three-member committee to examine the issue of rates, hold hearings, and make recommendations to the interior secretary for the establishment of an equitable rate policy for the railroad. This move would put the responsibility where it belonged and would enable him to attend to his own course of duties.

Ever skeptical, Ballaine soon found another way to throw the commission's management practices into question. This time he took issue with a March 1922 tariff agreement between the AEC and the Alaska Steamship Company establishing through rates from Seattle and Tacoma to destinations along the government railroad. When Ballaine got wind if this, he brought the matter to the attention of Alaska's new governor, Scott Bone, a former editor of the *Seattle Post Intelligencer* and an active participant in Harding's presidential campaign. Basing his projections on what little he knew, Ballaine claimed the rates were unfair and excessive. He accused the commission of further collusion because the rate divisions were agreed upon "in secret" with Alaska Steamship and, from all appearances, seemed to be extremely high.

When Governor Bone learned of this, he asked Mears to explain the validity of the allegations. Mears acknowledged that the commission's decision to keep the division of rates confidential had been made to avoid the kind of misinterpretation the governor had been exposed to. He explained in detail how the measurement basis for the rates had been agreed upon. Rather bluntly, he added that whoever had made the estimates quoted in the complaint had no knowledge of freight classifications. He then secured copies of the rate divisions for the governor and the attorney general with the caveat that, "Before additional conclusions regarding rates are sent abroad, a careful investigation of the facts be undertaken."

In the coming months, Ballaine would continue to publish erroneous and defamatory accounts about the AEC, contending that the railroad and the syndicate were throttling all of Alaska. Mears by then surely knew what to expect from the man and simply chose to let his own performance speak for itself.

## BEYOND THE CALL OF DUTY

Although the controversy about Mears' salary seemed to have been resolved, it would not rest. In March 1922, with the railroad nearing completion, the issue came up again. This time it took the form of a decision rendered by Lurtin Ginn, acting comptroller general under President Harding. Citing statutes dating back to 1894, Ginn claimed that Mears could not legally occupy or accept pay for his AEC position without vacating his army commission.

The act of March 12, 1914, Ginn said, had authorized the president to appoint officers only from the engineer corps of the army or navy to the commission and to fix the salaries of those appointed. It made no mention of extending that authority to include officers of the regular army. In particular, Ginn sought to disallow any payments to Mears since July 1, 1921 that would have effected an annual pay rate of $15,000, since no AEC employee was allowed more than $10,000.

Ginn refused to recognize the intent of Congress in drawing up the joint resolution of May 13, 1914, which had authorized the appointment of Mears by name. Its purpose was to supplement the March act and to legally empower the president to assign Mears to duty on the AEC without interfering with his army commission. Congress, the secretaries of war and interior, and Frederick Mears himself, all had viewed it with the understanding that the appointment would in no way adversely affect his status as an army officer. Yet, regardless of this understanding, Ginn found nothing in the joint resolution that would repeal the earlier statues or override the original act relating to officers of the engineer corps. "If the Congress," he said, "had intended to authorize the appointment of army officers to civil offices or positions in connection with the work in Alaska, or payment to them of additional compensation . . . specific provision to that effect would have been made in the act."

Throughout Mears' service in Alaska, disbursing officers of the army and the AEC had honored both acts from 1914, and made payments to him accordingly. Ginn questioned the practice. He maintained that accountants in the two agencies should have raised objections from the beginning.

This astonishing decision was delivered precisely as Mears arrived in Washington with Governor Bone to make preliminary arrangements for President Harding to visit the territory. One moment he was being feted by upwards of fifty congressmen and business moguls at the exclusive Racquet Club, enjoying an all-Alaska repast and receiving accolades about the commission's work. The next moment he was facing an attack that could throw his entire career into question. The record remains unclear as to why these two events coincided so tidily or why, indeed, Lurtin Ginn took on the task of investigating legislation relative to Mears' salary at all. Whoever was hoping to oust the man on the basis of those findings was ill-prepared for the force of the colonel's rebuttal.

Mears had endured many setbacks during his years with the railroad, but when the comptroller general's office firmly positioned itself to deny him his army commission, it was going too far. Furthermore, he was not about to let himself be deprived of the retirement privileges granted him after his eight years of service in the Canal Zone. Now it was due time, perhaps even past time, for Mears to take up the pen in his own defense.

The response he sent to Ginn twelve days later, with copies to Secretary Fall and Chairman Curry, included full documentation about the examinations he'd taken in connection with his various promotions in the army. These clearly identified "service in Alaska" among the orders he had been issued at each juncture of his army career. The essence of his statement reads:

> This matter is not the outcome of a few weeks or a few months: on the contrary, my Regular Army status has been recognized by both the War and Interior Departments from the inception of this work. Surely, in simple justice to me, if any question arose as to the nature of my Army status, I

should have been returned to active duty by Army order.

I have served in the Regular Army of the United States continuous since October 20, 1899, over twenty-two years. (My father similarly served in the Regular Army for over thirty years, and died in the service.)

I do not feel that, under the circumstances as I have related them, with the Army orders and the joint resolution of Congress protecting me, it should be held that I have vacated my commission in the Regular Army of the United States.

I stand ready to tender my resignation as chairman and chief engineer of the Alaskan Engineering Commission at any moment, provided the same would in any way facilitate my restoration to standing which I believe I am entitled in the Regular Army of the United States.

Congressman Curry's Committee on Territories held hearings on the matter, and Mears went before them dressed in full military attire. He was proud of his army connection and had nothing to hide. The aura of his presence at the hearings, together with the strength of his testimony, must have made that abundantly clear. If anything, the government had been in error. In their haste to get Mears to Alaska in 1914, Secretary Lane and others involved in drafting the necessary legislation had been too imprecise with their wording. As far as they were concerned at the time, all was in order. Everyone agreed with the intent of the language. As Curry put it, "I do not think it would be fair for us not to keep our contract with Mears which was made through the previous administration."

Suddenly Fall, who one year earlier had considered replacing the chairman with Ballaine, turned a right about-face in support of Mears. Apparently impressed with the earnestness of Mears' response, he might have been afraid that Mears would in fact resign, if his status with the army were not reconfirmed, leaving the AEC without a chairman. Siding with Curry that Mears had an arguable case, Fall wrote to the committee, "I will say without hesitation that I cannot agree with the decision of the Comptroller General as to Colonel Mears' status." Should the decision be allowed to stand, he said, "a very great and grave injustice will be done to a most meritorious officer and a gentleman who has rendered splendid service in the performance of his duties."

Fall drafted a new joint resolution to reinforce the original intent of Mears' appointment and to waive Ginn's findings. Secretary of War John Weeks amended the wording to make the resolution better protective of the status of Mears and other military officers who might follow him in the management of the railroad. It reaffirmed Mears' military standing and legally authorized payments that had been honorably and properly made to him. Weeks' statement accompanying the resolution attributed the current situation to "complications caused by the multiplicity of statutes affecting the availability of Army officers." The government, he said, had an overriding need for Mears' special qualifications in serving the public good. To correct any unfairness dealt the colonel, this resolution would acknowledge his "unquestioning response to the demands made upon him under his past and present assignments to duty." The bill, H.J. Res. 316, eventually passed both houses of Congress, but not until August of that year.

## FULL STEAM AHEAD

Setting his sights on finishing the work, but prepared to resign on the spot if necessary, Mears returned to Alaska that summer with renewed determination. Before he could buckle down to concentrate on the Tanana bridge, however, several pieces of deferred business required his attention.

One of these was a first-class hotel the AEC was building along the railroad right-of-way at mile 248.5. Under construction nearby were tennis courts, a swimming pool, and a three-hole golf course. These amenities would offer an added inducement for passengers wanting to spend the night in hopes of seeing Mount McKinley the next morning. Mears named it the Curry Hotel in honor of Charles Curry, the railroad's champion in Congress.

Two projects of importance to southcentral Alaska and Anchorage also needed Mears' involvement. The first had to do with a proposal by two Anchorage businessmen, Frank I. Reed and Robert Pope, to develop a hydroelectric station adjacent to the main line of the railroad. The other stemmed from the enabling act of 1914, which specified that the commission include the needs of the military in its planning.

The hydroelectric project, on the Eklutna River twenty-seven miles north of Anchorage, had previously been studied by the AEC's engineering department and had long been supported by the town's business community. After reviewing his earlier correspondence on the matter, Mears recommended to Fall that the Eklutna site be leased to the Federal Power Commission for possible development by private enterprise. The ensuing project became known as the Anchorage Power and Light Company. It was completed in 1929, after many years of fund raising by its promoters. Power that the railroad had previously supplied to Anchorage was phased out.

In a speech before the Anchorage Chamber of Commerce in July 1922, Mears reintroduced the mandate stipulating that the government's railroad benefit both civilian and military populations in Alaska. Informing the group that the army soon planned to close Fort Gibbon at the mouth of the Tanana River, and Fort Liscum near the town of Valdez, he asked them again to support the building of a permanent military post near Anchorage. It was obvious he favored the area for having "the best climate in the Territory where troops would be able to drill out-of-doors from the months of April to October." In time, two large military establishments, Fort Richardson and Elemendorf Air Force Base would be installed on the outskirts of Anchorage. Today they serve as a shield of defense, not only for the city, but for all of Alaska.

## CROSSINGS COMPLETE

At his first opportunity that same summer, Mears made a trip north to inspect the work of the crews who were building the 540-foot south approach span leading to the Tanana bridge. Almost as long as the bridge itself, this approach was an integral part of the overall design. Using huge cranes and all manner of equipment, workers built, aligned, and bolted together a series of heavy timbers to form the structure. Ever mindful of the admonishment to build with speed and economy, Mears would not compromise himself or the integ-

*BL79-1-297 Anchorage Museum of History and Art*

American Bridge Company engineers fabricated the Tanana River bridge from designs originally conceived by Mears.

*AEC G-2106 Anchorage Museum of History and Art*
Viewed here from the north bank, the bridge at Nenana was the final link in
the government railroad connecting the tidewaters of the Pacific to the interior
of Alaska.

rity of this project by rushing to completion a job that was meant
to last. He was building for permanency.

In late August, after the approach spans and concrete piers and
abutments were approved, crews of the American Bridge Company
began arriving at Nenana. By this time, all of the steel sections of the
bridge were on the ground at the building site. Men worked through
the rest of the summer and fall, installing the false work and then
swinging the massive segments into place. On November 23, 1922,
the first train crossed the bridge, even as crews continued securing
the framework high above the snow-covered track.

The following February, when the crossing was open to traffic, many compared it to the Chicago, Burlington and Quincy bridge
over the Ohio River at Metropolis, Illinois. The 720-foot channel
span of the Ohio bridge was thought at the time to be the world's

AEC G-2119 *Anchorage Museum of History and Art*

The Tanana River bridge opened to traffic in February 1923. Fifty-one years later it was named the Frederick Mears Memorial Bridge.

longest through truss single span. But the 700-foot steel span of the Tanana bridge, sweeping bank to bank over one of the largest navigable rivers of Alaska, was considered to be more dramatic.

The bridges were the most spectacular part of the entire project, and the Tanana bridge was its capstone. To all intents and purposes, the railroad was now open for business, although the existing narrow-gauge track between Nenana and Fairbanks had yet to be widened. Since there would be no advantage to standardizing the track in the middle of winter, Mears and his engineers put off that work until spring. Shoving apart those last seventy-five miles of rail meant that Mears would be parting company with the dinkey engines. In his mind's eye, he could still see the little ruffians breathing life into the project as they pulled tons of construction materials along track laid directly on the frozen

*Mears collection*

Construction of the Alaska Railroad took the power of locomotives, horses, and brute labor. Not a single motor truck was used.

tundra and provided essential engine power before tracks could be laid at all.

The year 1922 had been one of peaks and valleys, accomplishment and disillusionment for the AEC's chairman and chief engineer. Yet, as far as he was concerned, until the last spike was driven, celebrating completion of the railroad would be premature. The closer he came to that reality, the more he began seriously to consider what he would do next.

Back in April, the Mearses had observed their fifteenth wedding anniversary. As was his custom, Mears wrote a long poem to Jane, his "sweetheart, pal, and wife." This time he mused that simply to be together with her, sharing their love and their home, was enough. He saw the path ahead as smoother and less arduous than the grades they'd been climbing so far: "With our lives and our souls, let us mingle as one/We can smile at the future for the battle is won."

# ANCHORAGE TO PAY DUE HOMAGE TO COLONEL FREDERICK MEARS AT PUBLIC RECEPTION TONIGHT

**PUBLIC RECEPTION TONIGHT AT ELKS' TEMPLE IN HONOR OF COLONEL AND MRS. FREDERICK MEARS—ALL ANCHORAGE CORDIALLY INVITED—RECEPTION STARTS AT 10 P. M.—PROMINENT OFFICIAL LEAVING FOR STATES.**

All Anchorage is cordially invited to attend the public reception to be given tonight for Colonel Frederick Mears at the Elks' temple. This is distinctly a town affair to which the public is invited. Colonel Mears leaves tomorrow for Seward, en route to Seattle, where he will report for duty with the United States army.

As a private citizen perhaps Colonel Mears has been misjudged. In his position it was necessary to assume an attitude of dignity peculiar to the occasion. The position commanded respect and Colonel Mears wore the cloth of power in a manner creditable to himself, the administration and Alaskans. At that Colonel Mears is decidedly human; he is endowed with a splendid vein of humor; he is generous in thought and action, and is above all a "man's man," capable of acting a man's part and doing a man's work.

Naturally Colonel Mears has enemies, and in this he glories, as do all big men. He is a success and will continue to make a success of life. His home life is ideal and the exemplary manner of living his every day life is one worthy of emulation.

In Colonel Mears Anchorage loses a friend, a friend tried and true. But we do not lose him in spirit, for he has declared his allegiance to Anchorage and has voluntarily promised to work for

## CHAPTER 15

# THE GOLDEN SPIKE

*In this maze of conflicting interests, Colonel Mears has the lion's share of credit for an engineering project transcending that of the tunnel line from Geneva to Monte Carlo.*

*The Morning Oregonian*
July 16, 1923

Built at a cost of $56 million over a period of eight years, the Alaska Railroad finally reached completion by the summer of 1923. Preparations for President Harding's historic visit to the territory in June of that year were well underway when Anchorage Mayor M.J. Conroy received this letter from Alaska's governor:

My dear Mayor Conroy,

  The purser of the *Alameda* delivered to me this
morning the golden spike presented to Colonel Frederick Mears by the City of Anchorage. Please advise me as to the arrangements for the driving of
this spike.
  I hear there is a suggestion that Colonel Mears
be invited to become the guest of Anchorage during
the visit of the President and ceremonies incident to
the driving of the golden spike. This impresses me
as a very fitting thing to do and a very happy idea.

Very truly yours,
Scott C. Bone

Any casual observer of the situation would respond to such a
query that, *of course*, Colonel Mears should be present at the official
ceremony driving the golden spike. What is puzzling is that there
should ever have been any question about the matter. Why was the
colonel ignored at the crowning moment of his accomplishment?
The story of how this peculiar set of circumstances arose traces to
the political climate in Washington D.C. during 1923, and inevitably to John Ballaine.

## BLUNDERBUSS DECISIONS

  Congress learned in the waning summer of 1922 that valuable
tracts of the nation's naval oil reserves had been secretly leased to
wealthy entrepreneurs. An outspoken advocate for political reform,
"Fighting" Bob LaFollette, a senator from Wisconsin, asked why
Congress should not inquire, who were the real organizers to be

favored by the government "with a special privilege in value beyond the dreams of Croesus?" The ensuing investigation sought to prove that President Harding had given his consent to leasing those lands, according to terms drawn up by Secretary Fall. LaFollette said of Fall, "It would have been possible to pick a worse man for Interior but not altogether easy." Harding responded, "If Fall is not an honest man, then I am not fit to be President."

In the weeks and months that followed, major newspapers around the country began to editorialize about political immorality among national leaders and the voters. No one above or below ground was beyond the reach of innuendo. Standing by to exploit the situation was John Ballaine, who left no stone unturned in his vendetta to expose what he considered to be the "crimes" of the AEC. He resurrected everything he had ever written, published, and circulated about what he termed the "strangling" of the Alaska Railroad. Resorting to mendacious rhetoric, he repeatedly stated that the government railroad produced no revenue, lacked available coal, charged excessive freight rates, and was hampered by the silting up of Cook Inlet and by the Alaska Syndicate.

Soon the winds of investigation began reaching gale proportions. Proving the power of propaganda, Ballaine and his posturing succeeded in diverting the attention of many members of the worried Congress from the Teapot Dome crisis to his allegations about the AEC. Meanwhile, the Department of Commerce conducted its own examination of the records and found reasons to take pride in the AEC's performance. When compared to other per mile investments for U.S. railways, the cost per mile for construction of the Alaska Railroad did not appear out of line. The study provided hard evidence that the railroad in Alaska was already producing sizable revenues from passenger fares, freight hauls, baggage movement, express shipments and port fees. The overall report was optimistic, and its incompatibility with Ballaine's account only compounded Harding and Fall's problems. In shock over the political corruption surrounding him, and besieged with conflicting advice, Harding asked again and again what he should do.

And so it was at this stage of his presidency that Harding began to plan for a "voyage of understanding" across the United States. Bruised and bewildered, he would use the occasion of the trip to promote his reelection. He meant to tell the nation's people how he had been betrayed. He could only hope they would believe him and give him another chance.

Harding's transcontinental tour offered a perfect opportunity for him to visit the territory of Alaska and to be the first president ever to do so while in office. The year before, while in the nation's capital, Governor Bone and Colonel Mears had drawn up provisional arrangements for such a visit. Now these plans could take definite shape. The goal for this tour was for the president to travel the completed railroad and thereby see as much of the territory as possible.

The first leg of the itinerary would take Harding and his delegation aboard the naval vessel *Henderson* to Ketchikan, Alaska's first port of entry. The group would continue from there through the southeastern waters of the Inland Passage. Community leaders and descendants of the territory's indigenous people would be on hand to greet them along the way. Upon arrival in the capital city of Juneau, President Harding and his wife, Florence, would attend a formal dinner at the governor's mansion, hosted by Governor and Mrs. Bone. A large outdoor reception and dance for over three hundred people would follow.

After sailing across the Gulf of Alaska to Seward, the party would board the government railroad and travel the full 470 miles to the interior, with a stop at McKinley National Park. The eleven-car "Presidential Special" featured two business cars, three sleepers, a diner, a smoking car, and two observation cars. One of these had originally rolled with the Great Northern Railway's "Orient Express" between Minneapolis and Seattle. The culmination of the tour would be the site of the Tanana River bridge, where Harding would drive a ceremonial spike to signify the completion of the transportation project.

Harding had every reason to want to part company with his sordid past but had neither the courage nor the nerve to fire his former friends. Fall spared him that indignity: to avoid having his own reputation wholly discredited in that manner, he announced in January that he would quit the cabinet in March.

Fall believed the lack of development in Alaska could be overcome by stimulating traffic and that what the railroad needed was a promoter. Often he had stressed it was time to eliminate the AEC, reorganize the project, give it a new name and appoint another manager. For the most part, his attempts to reorganize the administration of Alaska had failed. Although he'd succeeded in moving the Government Land Office from Juneau to Anchorage, he had effected little else. In a feverish, last-minute effort to resuscitate his image—and under the ruse of doing something good for Alaska and its people—Fall obtained Harding's approval for consolidating the activities of the Alaska Engineering Commission and the Alaska Road Commission.

## THE LAST STRAW

Mears was away from Anchorage when he received the news. Up north, workers were having to wait until spring before they could install the standard-gauge track between Nenana and Fairbanks. Mears was spending the majority of that time in Seattle, negotiating with the Alaska Steamship Company. His mission was to establish freight rates comparable to the AEC's for other government bureaus in Alaska. He was also there to work out rates for coal shipments to Nome and to points on the Yukon River from mines along the railroad. Aware of impending change within the Department of Interior, surely Mears wondered what his role would be in Fall's new organizational plan.

The answer came on February 13, when new army orders arrived, tersely relieving him of his station and duties with the AEC and reassigning him to the Third Division headquartered in Seattle. That same day came an equally officious directive from Fall stating that Mears' position was being subsumed by James G. Steese, a full colonel with the Army Corps of Engineers, who had been serving as chairman of the Alaska Road Commission since 1920. Fall's blunt notice implied clearly that Mears was to complete the transfer of the AEC business to Steese as expeditiously as possible; the army orders stipulated a deadline of May 1.

That Mears had not been included in the transition planning only added to the insult. Early in 1922, he had suggested that the two commissions be placed under the aegis of the War Department. But Fall, with only one month left before his resignation, was consumed with trying to whitewash his own reputation quickly by combining the two transportation agencies. Now, with room for only one manager of the new entity, his choices were few. The fact that Steese already possessed some railroad knowledge gave him the advantage over Mears, who had no comparative road experience. In Fall's haste to carry out the transition, he failed to give common courtesy to the man who had served as chief overseer of the railroad since its inception.

Mears returned to Anchorage in late February to begin clearing out his desk. On the eve of the railroad's completion, transferring the mantle of the AEC could not have been an altogether enjoyable task. Nor was it a simple one. Mears had an obligation to inform Steese about the makeshift solutions he'd employed during the course of the commission's work and under less than favorable circumstances. Although the AEC had laid a foundation for permanency, the railroad would continue to require significant and costly upgrading. Contrary to Fall's wishful thinking, what lay ahead for the project involved much more than routine operation.

## A GIFT FROM ANCHORAGE

To the end of his service with the railroad, Mears held the loyalty and trust of his former employees. He'd been with them from the beginning of the tent town on the mud flats through the early construction boom and the incorporation of Anchorage. It was a bond of memory and association that insured a sympathetic hearing whenever an old resident had a problem or grievance. No such bond existed between the railroad employees, the community, and Steese. While most of the people were prepared eventually to part company with Mears, they were saddened, even angered, when the natural order of his departure was altered so abruptly.

Mears' older daughters, now in their teens, saw their father's dismissal as a great humiliation to both of their parents, especially in light of all they had endured and accomplished in Alaska. A scene recounted by Betty underscores the intensity of emotion that prevailed in those weeks. When Colonel Steese, trim and neatly groomed, approached Jane with a farewell bouquet of flowers, she refused to accept them. Abandoning her usual gracious manner, she looked him straight in the eye and said, "Colonel Steese, I see no reason why I should speak to you at all." To her mind, he represented the government that had ousted her husband.

Before leaving Alaska for the last time, the Mearses attended gatherings held in their honor at Fairbanks and Nenana where they were surrounded with spontaneous expressions of good will and friendship. Keenly alive to the benefits the railroad had bestowed upon their town, the citizens of Nenana commended Colonel Mears for his assistance in making their community the railroad's connecting link to river steamer service of the interior and for turning over to their little city its light plant, telephone system, and fire department.

People in general shared the opinion that perhaps Mears had been misjudged. An editorial in the *Anchorage Daily Times* concluded that, in his position, it was necessary to assume an "attitude of dignity peculiar to the occasion." The position commanded respect, the writer continued, and Mears "wore the cloth in a manner creditable to himself, the administration, and all Alaskans. Those who knew him well saw that he was decidedly human, endowed with a splendid sense of humor, capable of acting a man's part and doing a man's work." With this, the newspaper extended an open invitation for all residents to attend a reception in his honor that very evening.

Anchorage wanted to give due recognition to the departing AEC chairman for practically giving them a well-organized town. On the night of the farewell event, everyone's attention centered on the colonel and his wife for the presentation of gifts. Members of the Anchorage Woman's Club had chosen beautifully hand-carved Alaska ivory jewelry for Jane. Then Andrew Christensen presented Mears with a golden spike, which had been purchased by popular subscription among the town's citizens.

Resting in a velvet box, the spike was inscribed with these words: "To Colonel Frederick Mears, who built the Alaska Railroad from Seward to Fairbanks, from the people of Anchorage." As Mears read the inscription, he looked older than his forty-five years. His hair was thinning now, and his face, creased with strain, cut a fuller profile than it had nine years ago—a testament to the rigors of his assignment and the unpredictability of his foes, both natural and political.

Thanking Christensen and all of the townspeople, Mears predicted a brilliant future for Anchorage and for the Alaska Railroad. He asked everyone to support Colonel Steese in the same way they had supported him. Wishing them farewell, Mears expressed deep regrets for leaving Anchorage at this time but acknowledged his duty in accepting the mandates of higher authority.

The golden spike which Mears received that evening was the one he later handed over to the purser of the *Alameda* for delivery to Scott Bone. The governor's hope that Mears be included at the presidential ceremony would not be fulfilled, however. The appearance of the spike on that day, bearing its commemoration of Mears, seems to have been the colonel's own quiet way of being present for the event.

## THE CEREMONY

Less than three months after Mears' departure from Alaska, locomotive No. 618 rolled out of Seward with the Harding delegation on board. Traveling with the president and his wife were several cabinet members, including Secretary of Commerce Herbert Hoover, Secretary of Agriculture Henry Wallace, and the secretaries of the army and navy. Also in the group was the new Secretary of Interior, Hubert Work.

A rotund, white-haired, kindly looking man, Work had been serving as postmaster general when Harding named him to the position vacated by Albert Fall. Before announcing Work's appointment, Harding had repudiated the former secretary's organizational policies for Alaska and had promised new direction within the Department of Interior. At the golden spike ceremony, Work would speak as the representative of the department which had overseen construction and financing of the government railroad from its inception.

Afterwards Work and Hoover were to hold hearings in Fairbanks relative to the widespread reports about mismanagement and overexpenditures by the AEC. They were determined to get to the bottom of the matter. By this time, Ballaine's allegations had mushroomed. He was blaming government officials for yielding to the "contagion" of Anchorage in its determination to make itself the capital of Alaska and the territory's public, economic, and social center. In addition, he demanded an administrative investigation because freight from Fairbanks was being trans-shipped to the Guggenheims' steamship line from Anchorage, eliminating use of the government's own railroad to carry the freight south to his port city of Seward.

Harding's entourage had an opportunity to show their impartiality when Ballaine boldly attempted to board the president's train as it was leaving Seward. By this time, the group was all too familiar with the man's activities as self-appointed investigator of the AEC, and they swiftly rebuffed him. They had enough to deal with and were not willing to allow this apparent rabble-rouser an opportunity to create more trouble for the president.

The long journey north gave the visiting dignitaries ample time to witness and comprehend the full extent of the AEC's accomplishments in the raw land of Alaska. No chief executive could fail to appreciate the know-how and sheer determination of those who had directed the effort. The train ride in itself was a form of vindication for Mears. At every stop, railroad workers expecting to greet the colonel expressed disappointment that he was not there. Somewhere between Seward and Nenana, evidently, or perhaps earlier, the president and his companions acknowledged that not to have included Mears in the ceremonial festivities was an egregious oversight. They realized they were obliged to soften the implications of Fall's actions and to give Mears due recognition as best they could in his absence.

The Presidential Special pulled into Nenana on the afternoon of July 15, after an exhausting series of speeches and honorary events along the way. News reporters, photographers, and a host of residents and railroad workers, looking crisp and dignified in their Sunday best, were there to welcome the president when he arrived. Although noticeably tired from his 4,000-mile cross-country journey, as well as from the heat of the interior, Harding rose to the occasion to greet the people.

The sun bore down as the crowd gathered around the north end of the Tanana bridge, the site of the ceremony. With his wire spectacles perched askew at the end of his nose, Secretary Work opened his remarks by observing that, when the railroad project began, no one could have foreseen that the nation's chief executive would drive the last spike. Praising the hardy workmen "who suffered cold and defied death that they might write their page in history," Work proudly presented their accomplishment to the president.

He then gave a special commendation to Colonel Mears, whose construction, character, and conception of service were "without flaw." As every great achievement is but the shadow of a man, he said, so is the Alaska Railroad the shadow of this intrepid engineer. The secretary expressed gratitude on the government's behalf for the colonel's trustworthy service in expending $56 million in a wild country, with little supervision, and without avoidable error.

"This great builder," he stated, "clearly has woven himself into the fabric of the railroad and enshrined in the hearts of the Alaska people the name of Frederick Mears."

Finally, offering the trophy for all to see, he gave it to the president saying,

> In tribute to your known sympathy for the hopes of Alaskans, Colonel Mears wishes that you may drive this golden spike, presented him by the people of Anchorage, and rivet the tie that will bind Alaska's commercial relations to the United States.

President Harding added words of his own in thanks to the pioneers who'd had the courage to build this steel highway "through an almost impassable land." Short of mentioning Mears by name, he continued,

> The outstanding genius of it all is the man who found the way, who had the conception, the perception, and the confidence to find an open pathway through the mountains, the wilderness, and canyons, to surmount the various other physical difficulties which necessarily had to be encountered.

At the close of his speech, Harding said, "In my humble judgment, the qualities of the pioneers cooperating with the transportation line . . . will do more to work out the development of this wonderful land than anything which the great government of the United States can do."

With that, Governor Bone positioned the golden spike, and the president hammered it gently. Then a permanent iron substitute was quickly set in its place. Long out of practice and physically weak, Harding missed twice before finally driving the spike into the tie. This dramatic moment, resounding with shouts and tears of joy, marked the official completion of the railroad, linking the waters of the Pacific to the interior of Alaska.

At the conclusion of the festivities, Harding retreated to the comfort of his private car to ride the final fifty-six miles of line north out of Nenana. The entire tour had allowed him to experience the matchless scenery of Alaska, from the lofty mountain peaks to the forested valleys rich with vegetation. It gave him a wealth of material to draw from in upcoming speeches about further development of the territory. When the train arrived in Fairbanks at nine o'clock that evening, the summer sun was still shining.

*B75 134-186 Anchorage Museum of History and Art*

President Warren G. Harding pounds the golden spike at the Tanana River bridge near Nenana, July 15, 1923. Inscribed to Colonel Mears from the people of Anchorage, the golden spike symbolized completion of the government railroad in Alaska.

## AROUND THE NEXT BEND

In the next day's press coverage of the event, west coast newspapers carried extensive stories about what they referred to as the "trouble" in Alaska. Acknowledging that Mears deserved a major share of the credit for successful completion of the railroad, news writers pointed out that the colonel "was not present for the greater personal recognition which he rightly might have expected for his years of service against great odds." His friends, they added, were "very bitter over his reassignment on the eve of the hour of his triumph."

In anticipation of the Hoover-Work hearings in Fairbanks, the same news stories recounted Ballaine's perennial complaints about official corruption, capitalistic influence, political wire-pulling, and administrative blundering, which were allegedly costing American taxpayers millions of dollars. Because the word "bribery" had not yet been used, however, the *San Francisco Chronicle* chose to wait and see whether formal charges would be made as a result of the hearings.

The outcome, in short, was that Ballaine suffered another defeat. President Harding emerged from the land of the midnight sun recanting any negative feelings he had once held about the government railroad there and envisioning great promise for all of Alaska. On July 27, speaking before 60,000 people at the University of Washington football stadium, he extolled Alaska's great potential and committed the government to using the railroad aggressively in developing the land.

Part way through the address, however, he dropped his prepared speech and grasped the lectern in a momentary lapse of consciousness. Hoover quickly collected the scattered sheets and put them back in order for the president. Harding then managed to regain his composure enough to finish his remarks.

Visibly shaken from his exhaustive travel, Harding chose to rest in San Francisco before attempting to return to the capital. On July 28, he suddenly became ill, and he died five days later. While the cause of death was reputed to be embolism, newspaperman William A. White wondered, "how the doctors could diagnose an illness that was part terror, part shame, and part utter confusion!"

Albert Fall had walked away from his post believing that what he had set in motion in Alaska would result in an economical solution to the government's costly transportation concerns there. But that stratagem, too, proved to be ill-fated. In addition to consolidating railroad improvements with ongoing road construction, Colonel Steese served as director of public works throughout the territory and as consulting engineer for the sixteenth lighthouse district. Although well suited to his new job, Steese became overloaded with responsibilities in no time. Six months after his appointment, he was replaced. After that, all efforts to unify the Alaska Road Commission and the Alaska Engineering Commission came to an end.

For his part, Hubert Work saw to it that the remnants of the organization that had been the AEC were renamed "The Alaska Railroad." The entity continued to function marginally for years. Finally, in 1938, it began operating at a profit under the directorship of Otto Ohlson, another army man with a strong background of railroad experience.

John Ballaine's prolific writings about unfair dealings in the territory culminated in his self-published tract, "The Strangling of the Alaska Railroad," in 1923. His prominence faded with the dissolution of the AEC, and he is best remembered today as Seward's founder, the man who gave the town its name. Mid-January 1941, he suffered an inglorious death in Seattle at the age of seventy-two. True to form until the end, he supplied newspapers in advance with his own obituary.

Commenting in retrospect, Congressman Charles Curry described Colonel Mears' dismissal as simply a matter of politics. Had Mears striven to be more of a promoter and developer, his story might have turned out differently. Surely upon completion of the railroad, Mears would have enjoyed sharing in the glory of a job well done. But, just as surely, he must have had little interest in spending any more time at the mercy of those for whom he lacked respect. His papers give no indication that he believed his chairmanship to be anything more than a position of high responsibility and temporary tenure. Such was the way of the army.

The moment of the family's departure from Anchorage, in May 1923, left a vivid impression in young Betty's memory. In her words, "It was a wrenching experience for all of us. A seething mass of people standing on the wharf were crying and waving as our ship moved out to sea. We were weeping as well. There was not a dry eye."

The inscribed golden spike would eventually find its way back from Nenana into the colonel's possession, but Frederick Mears would never again set foot on Alaska soil.

**CHAPTER 16**

# ONCE AN ENGINEER
# ALWAYS AN ENGINEER

*When a man dies, the world asks not who were his*
*antecedents, or how much money did he have, but*
*what has he done.*

Frederick Mears to his children

Mears' time with the army was short-lived after he left Alaska and settled the family in a waterfront home across Puget Sound from Seattle. There they lived during that bittersweet summer, swimming, digging clams, and running with their dogs. As usual, they were quite a sufficient family unit. No longer bound by the political constraints that had plagued his every move, Mears was now free to set another course for his life.

He had often considered retiring from the military to work in the private sector, and the fact that he had finished his tenure with the AEC presented an opportunity for potential employers to seek him out. First to step forward was the board of the St. Paul Depot Company, which was owned by a consortium of nine railroads. Most of the board members were acquainted with the caliber of Mears' work and some of them had served with him in Panama or in France. Mears' longtime associate Ralph Budd was now president of the depot company as well as president of the Great Northern Railway. The job he offered Mears brought with it solid assurances for future work with the burgeoning Great Northern. It was exactly the kind of job Mears had hoped to find. He resigned from the army as a full colonel in the corps of engineers on July 7, 1923—just one week before the driving of the golden spike in Alaska.

Within a month, Mears received a note from General Pershing acknowledging his retirement. In simple words, Pershing thanked him for his many years of faithful service and wished him health and prosperity in his new sphere of life. The sincerity of the message was gratifying. It echoed the expression of appreciation Mears might have received from his superiors in Washington, had the circumstances been different.

## COMING FULL CIRCLE

Things turned out well for the Mearses, almost in accord with Pershing's salutations. This time, there was no contention about Mears' activities among those funding the job or in the press. His returning to work again with those who had employed him twenty-six years before brought enjoyable changes for the whole family. Toward summer's end, they bought a big, rambling frame house in St. Paul. Life was different for them there than it had been in Anchorage. The lilacs surrounding the house revived the interest

Jane had always had in gardening; Betty and Jo wore nautical blouses and skirts to a fashionable girls' prep school in the city.

The project in St. Paul was the construction of a $15 million modern passenger station and accompanying track layout for the nine owners' railroads. The previous chief engineer for the project had died, and Mears was hired to replace him. Mears undertook the project with the same vitality and enthusiasm that had always characterized his efforts. He turned over the completed depot in less than the scheduled time. Years later, the city restored the elaborate structure, which has since received landmark status.

Before long, the family returned to Seattle, where they purchased a large house overlooking Lake Washington. This would be the last home Mears inhabited. From here, he continued his work for Great Northern, capping his career with another monumental achievement.

*Courtesy Minnesota Historical Society Library*

The St. Paul union depot, completed under Mears' supervision, is no longer an active railroad station, but the city continues to appreciate its nobility.

## THE TUNNEL AND THE SUMMIT

Since 1890, the president of the Great Northern, James J. Hill, had envisioned his line making the trip from Lake Superior to the Pacific coast in shorter distance and less time than any of the other existing transcontinental railways. The Cascade Mountains of Washington formed the last major obstacle to reaching that goal. Hill had been fortunate to have John Stevens, the "Hero of Lost Marias Pass," still in his employ back then and had dispatched him to conduct another investigation. Today the area along the route he located is known as Stevens Pass.

Because it involved steep terrain and multiple switchbacks, the Cascade Mountain route invariably had failed to meet Great Northern's performance standards over the years. After the war, therefore, the railway company authorized a new project, on Thanksgiving Day 1925, to honor the memory of Hill and one of his life's dreams: a long, straight tunnel through those mountains. Its length would be just short of eight miles, making it the longest tunnel on the North American continent at that time. Ralph Budd named Mears engineer-in-charge for the project under J. R.W. Davis, chief engineer for the railroad company. Mears would have to press hard; he had little more than three years to finish.

Work on the tunnel began in early December. The plan was to drill through from both ends at the same time. In addition, a deep shaft was dug from the valley directly above the work area to an intermediate point within the tunnel. This and a smaller pioneer tunnel built parallel to the main bore would allow other workers to excavate from multiple faces simultaneously. Nearly 1,800 laborers worked around the clock, every day for thirty-five months, until the openings met three thousand feet underground and four miles from the west portal.

So accurately had Mears and his staff made their calculations that the alignment was perfect to within a few inches. The tunnel was completed in just under the projected time, and its construction set an excavation record. It would pay for itself by greatly re-

Colonel Mears (second from right) with engineers and officers of the Great Northern Railway at the east portal of the Cascade Tunnel, January 12, 1929. Many considered the tunnel to be Mears' finest engineering achievement.

ducing the grades on the line, eliminating curvature, and shaving hours off the running time. It is so straight that a person can see daylight from the entrance all the way to the far end. At 7.79 miles in length, it was then the fifth longest tunnel in the world.

For Mears, the construction of the Cascade Tunnel was a professional triumph. It was the achievement for which he became widely recognized among his fellow engineers. Budd later said, "In many ways, and possibly in every way, this, more than any other single project, should stand as a monument to Colonel Mears' engineering ability. . . . He personally supervised the engineering work and deserves the credit for its successful execution."

On January 12, 1929, a remarkable dedication ceremony took place. The National Broadcasting Company carried the event live by radio over thirty-eight network stations nationwide, with parts of the ceremony broadcast from widely separate locations. Millions listened as the Great Northern's "Oriental Limited" approached the east portal at Berne, where Ralph Budd was standing by to dedicate the new tunnel. He and the emcee boarded there for the train's maiden trip through. Also aboard were Mears and Stevens, along with other railroad officials, and the governor of Washington. While they rode, President-elect Herbert Hoover addressed the country from Washington D.C., and General Atterbury, once Mears' commanding officer in France and now president of the Pennsylvania Railroad, spoke from Philadelphia. George Olson and his orchestra provided musical interludes from New York, and celebrated vocalist Madame Schumann-Heink sang from studios in San Francisco.

When the train emerged from the west portal at Scenic station, the radio announcer gave a colorful account of the trip. A celebration banquet for upwards of six hundred jubilant guests ended the evening there. When Frederick Mears and John Stevens shook hands on this occasion, it was as equals: both of them had made railroad history.

The colonel remained with the Great Northern another eight years and through the Great Depression. Past fifty by this time, he continued to be productive throughout the period. One of his assignments was to supervise improvement and replacement of western portions of the line, including its 235-mile extension from Bend, Oregon, to Bieber, California. But nothing could top what he'd already accomplished. Mears had made his mark.

By 1937, his notoriety had spread to Europe, and he began receiving offers for consulting positions abroad. Traveling as a civilian, Mears had the opportunity to inspect the Simplon Tunnel through Mount Leone, on the border between Switzerland and Italy. Extending more than twelve miles, it was the longest tunnel in the world at the time and, excepting the English Channel Tunnel, remains the longest in Europe.

Mears' last major project was to make a thorough survey and report of the snow-retard work on the Austrian State Railway near Innsbruck, Austria, and on the Bernese Alps Railway near the nine-mile-long Loetschberg Tunnel in Switzerland. Nearing sixty, he still had the vigor to personally scale the mountains at those two sites. From the summit, he took many photographs to illustrate his findings. His detailed report of that work was his final outstanding contribution to engineering.

## CEDAROC

While the family had adapted themselves to city living, and Jane had resumed her civic involvement in Seattle, there was still a bit of Alaska in their hearts. An ongoing project for them since their days in St. Paul was construction and enjoyment of a vacation retreat in Montana. At every opportunity, Mears took time out to work on the house, with the help of his children and friends. The two-story log cabin overlooked Lake McDonald in Glacier

*Mears collection*

Cedaroc
After Mears retired from the military, the family built this retreat overlooking
Lake McDonald in Glacier Park, Montana.

Park. Accessible from the Great Northern line, it was not far
from Marias Pass. They called the place "Cedaroc." Though
smaller in scale, its design was similar to that of vacation homes
in the Adirondacks dating from the early 1900s.

While they built it, the family lived in tents, reminiscent of
their first summer in Anchorage. The cabin was rustically furnished with Native American rugs and baskets that the grandparents had collected at their military outposts. The colonel's hunting
trophies decorated the walls. One distinct recollection of Betty's
was watching black bears rummage around the property. Mears
frequently took the family along on rigorous treks and horseback
rides to the spectacular mountains and glaciers of the park. The
grandeur of the country never failed to evoke memories of the
great outdoors of Alaska.

Jane Mears at Glacier Park with daughter Helen.

*Mears collection*

Mears, nearing 60, and Jane at Cedaroc.

Those happy times together were shattered irretrievably
when Helen, the youngest, contracted bone cancer. She endured
for a year but died in 1929 at the age of twelve. In her last days,
Helen played "Janeen I Dream of Lilac Time" repeatedly on the
Victrola. Following her death, Mears could not bear to hear the
song again. Vivid in Betty's memory was the scene where, on hearing the music, her father burst into tears and turned it off.

Although things were never the same for the close-knit family after that loss, the vacation home continued to serve as a memorable refuge for the Mearses' grown children and their cousins. Jane eventually sold Cedaroc to the National Park Service for use as a ranger station. Later still, the cabin was moved to another site within the environs of the park by a young forester who refinished the logs and the interior for his own enjoyment.

## THE END OF THE LINE

In conjunction with the colonel's professional travels, Jane and son Frederick, a 1937 Yale graduate, accompanied Mears on a trip to Europe. The highlight was a nostalgic visit to Tours and Saumur. There, he could show Jane much of what he'd written about in his wartime letters from France. Again, the timing was perfect; the simmering hostilities in Europe had not yet erupted.

Colonel Mears would not live to see World War II. The bouts of pneumonia he'd suffered decades earlier in Alaska had taken their toll. At age sixty, when the disease struck again and his defenses were down, he lost the battle. The date was January 11, 1939, almost ten years to the day after the Cascade Tunnel dedication. That had been his crowning moment. Still, it was Jane's feeling that, despite the glory surrounding the tunnel project, Mears had enjoyed and valued his work in Alaska most of all.

Memorial services were conducted by Mears' close friend and confidant, Rev. Peter Trimble Rowe, first Bishop of the Episcopal Mission in Alaska, and by Dr. John McLaughlin, pastor of St. Mark's Episcopal church of Seattle. His older brother, Ned, and sister, Winifred, survived him. Betty comforted the family with her philosophy, "To live in the hearts of those who love you is not to die."

In a personal remembrance, gained from a lifetime's association with Mears, Ralph Budd captured the essence of the man's personality:

*Mears collection*

Colonel Mears remained active in engineering until
his death in 1939.

As an engineer and executive, Colonel Mears
always had a broad view of "the job" and allowed
nothing to interfere with it. He often exacted hard
service of the men under him, but was so reasonable
and kind that he never incurred their resentment.
Throughout his life he stood for the highest and finest in human relationship. . . . The power of his splendid mind, his entire lack of egotism, his absolute
honesty of thought and purpose, and his real kindli-
ness and tolerance never failed in their effect upon
those with whom he worked or played. A quiet sense
of fun shone through his apparent seriousness to
endear him to all who really knew him.

The colonel's spirit might have been shaken had he lived to witness the sad fate of his only son. Bearing a strong resemblance to his father and following the colonel's military ambitions, young Frederick went on to become a Naval Air Corps torpedo plane pilot in World War II. For his courage and success at Guadalcanal in October 1942, he won the Distinguished Flying Cross. But his fortune changed before he could receive the medal. Within a matter of months after his return to the U.S., Frederick was killed in a

*Mears collection*

Frederick Mears III, shown here holding the colonel's grandson Frederick Mears Meiggs, became a naval pilot and was decorated for his courage at Guadalcanal shortly before his death in 1943.

plane crash on a routine mission near the border between California and Mexico. He was twenty-seven years old. *Carrier Combat*, the book he wrote about his wartime experiences, was published posthumously in 1944.

Losing her son so soon after her husband, left an empty hollow in Jane's life. Not long after young Frederick's death, she moved from Seattle to Bel Air, California, where she lived with Betty and her  son, also named Frederick. During the ten years they lived together, Jane looked after the care of her grandson and financed his education at Shattuck Military Academy, the same institution his grandfather and great-grandfather had attended.

Heavy was the hand of war upon Jane, who bravely faced her losses as had her mother and her mother-in-law, Elizabeth MacFarland Mears, before her. She grieved deeply at the death of her brother, Jonathan "Skinny" Wainwright, who had been very much a part of her life and beloved among her family.

This was the same Jonathan Wainwright who, as a four-star general, had received a hero's welcome in New York City in 1945. His brave but hopeless stand on Bataan at Corregidor gave General MacArthur time to muster his forces in Australia at a critical turning point in the war. Thereafter, Wainwright endured three years of imprisonment by the Japanese. He'd had a chance to fly out with a plane sent to retrieve endangered nurses, but had chosen instead to remain with the men who had fought beside him so long and hard.

Jane was in poor health after Jonathan's death in July 1953. She died suddenly of a heart attack the following December. The Christmas carols she loved to sing were playing softly on the hospital intercom as she passed away. Jane is buried next to her husband in a small, beautifully wooded military cemetery at Fort Lawton near Seattle.

Both girls graduated from Vassar in the early 1930s. Jo married a doctor, John McVay, and bore two daughters. The family occupied the Mears home on Lake Washington for much of their lives. Jo died in 1965 of a heart condition that had kept her bedridden for many years. Her daughter, Marilyn McVay Richards, resided in Anchorage for nearly two decades before returning to the Seattle area.

Betty chose a more cosmopolitan life. After graduating in 1932, she worked as a copy writer for two years and then traveled the world. She married Henry Meiggs of New York, but he soon proved unfaithful. She divorced him after the birth of their son and moved west. In 1945, she joined the writing staff of NBC. Throughout her career as a television and screen writer, she was held in high respect by her colleagues and received numerous awards for her writing.

Frederick Mears Meiggs, the colonel's only grandson, lived in Hollywood. Instead of taking up a military career, he chose to pursue writing, as his mother had done. Both his grandparents were spared the knowledge that he, too, would die before his time as the result of an automobile accident in 1975. Thirty-three and single, the youngest Frederick left no offspring.

In her later years, Betty became the family historian. She served in that capacity until the end of her life. The last of Mears' children, she died in Hollywood at the age of eighty-two.

## MEARS REMEMBERED

Few Alaskans today recognize the name Frederick Mears or appreciate his contribution to their state's history, though evidence of his accomplishments abounds. Residents of Anchorage know of his wife because one of the city's first junior high schools was named for her in recognition of her efforts on behalf of all school children in the town's early days. Twenty years after construction of the original Jane Mears Junior High School in 1965, a new structure was built to accommodate growing student populations.

Anchorage missed an opportunity to honor the memory of Colonel Mears when developers suggested in the early 1970s that the city move his former residence, AEC House No. 29, to a different location instead of allowing it to be demolished. A committee of interested citizens took the initiative to verify the historical significance of the house and found it to be eligible for preservation as a landmark. Unfortunately, the municipality lacked the resources necessary to take action in time to save the structure from the wrecker's ball.

The U.S. Army honored Frederick Mears' service in Alaska by dedicating one of its posts to his memory during World War II. Fort Mears was built at Dutch Harbor in the Aleutian Islands during the summer of 1941, when the U.S. was fortifying its westernmost defenses in Alaska. A sizable naval air base was being established there at that time, and the army garrison was built to defend it. The dedication took place in September of that year.

At its peak, the number of troops stationed at Fort Mears reached 10,000. In the early days of June 1942, six months after

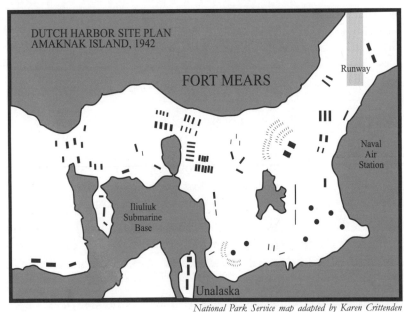

*National Park Service map adapted by Karen Crittenden*

The U.S. Army built Fort Mears at Dutch Harbor, Alaska, to defend the naval air station and submarine base there during World War II.

the bombing of Pearl Harbor, the Japanese attacked Dutch Harbor with ferocious air strikes. Many of the buildings at Fort Mears were damaged or destroyed. Some were repaired or replaced. Following the war, and after the army vacated the area and declared its property there surplus, most of the buildings stood empty for years.

Today, only "footprints" identify where buildings of the fort once stood. In 1998, the City of Unalaska broke ground to build the Museum of the Aleutians at Dutch Harbor. The purpose of the museum is to preserve the culture of the Aleutian peoples and to promote awareness about the region's history. The building stands on the foundation of what was once a warehouse within Fort Mears.

A second lasting tribute to Colonel Mears can be found at the site of the Tanana River bridge. There, on August 22, 1974, some fifty-one years after the driving of the golden spike at that spot, the Alaska Railroad dedicated the bridge itself to his name. Officiating at the ceremony, Alaska Railroad manager Walker Johnson gave a brief review of the important role the colonel had played in constructing the railroad. He then introduced Mears' granddaughter, Marilyn Richards of Anchorage, who unveiled the bronze plaque affixed to the massive steel structure. The inscription formally designates it the Frederick Mears Memorial Bridge.

When Thomas Riggs said of Mears that the man's worst fault was his modesty, he was probably right. Yet the colonel's legacy demonstrates that he was a man of honor and a true statesman, dedicated to proving the potential of the north. He pursued his work, not for personal gain, but for the benefit and enjoyment of future generations. Borrowing from Kipling in his memorial address about Mears, Ralph Budd observed, "He could walk with kings nor lose the common touch."

Former Governor Scott Bone of Alaska once stated that England had knighted captains of industry for achievements less magnificent and enduring than the completion of the Alaska Railroad. The project had involved infinitely greater difficulties than those encountered by the builders of the country's transcontinental rail lines. Today, as the twenty-first century opens, Americans pause to celebrate those who made important contributions to the nation's progress. This moment in history provides an opportunity for Colonel Frederick Mears to receive his rightful place among all the others who, in the words of Governor Bone, "have won niches in the halls of fame and will ever be held dear to American memory."

# NOTES

All information about Mears' personal life, his family, and his relatives derives from his private collection, which was given to me by his daughter Betty Wainwright Mears-Meiggs to use at my discretion, and from my correspondence with her, 1988-1990.

The family also granted me permission to access Mears' military records and those of his father housed at the military reference branch of the National Archives, Washington, D.C., and at the U.S. Military History Institute in Carlisle, Pennsylvania.

William Wilson generously gave me unlimited use of the material in his book *Railroad in the Clouds: The Alaska Railroad in the Age of Steam* (Pruett, 1977).

## CHAPTER 1—The Right Man for Alaska

Serving as the family historian, Betty Wainwright Mears-Meiggs was able to supply many of the details about Frederick Mears Sr. and Elizabeth McFarland Mears from the family archives and from her own recollections of family stories. Other sources included official military records and Mears' own collection of newspaper clippings. William Wilson's *Railroad in the Clouds* and his research collection, housed at the University of Alaska Rasmuson Library in Fairbanks, provided much of the background material on the Alaska Engineering Commission for this and later chapters.

"for the service and development of the country and its people": *Congressional Record*, 63d Cong., 2d sess., 1913, 51, pt. 1:76.

"Get Mears!": Ashmun Brown, "Man Who Will Build Alaskan Railroad Has Twice Won Success," *New York Press*, 31 May 1914.

living conditions at Omaha Barracks: Page and Meachim, *Descriptions of Military Posts*, 363-66; Greguras, *The History of the Post of Omaha*.

The city of Omaha had only one edifice: Wallace Stegner, *Angle of Repose* (Doubleday, 1971), 72.

Birth records: Frederick Mears' name occasionally appears in print with a middle initial inserted. Sometimes the initial is *J*, after his father's name; sometimes an *M* or a *C* is used. His birth certificate, however, indicates no middle name, nor does any of his correspondence.

Gonzaga Preparatory School: Fr. Neill R. Meany S.J., Archivist at Gonzaga University in Spokane, Washington, confirmed by correspondence that, for one year from 1892-1893, Frederick Mears attended Second Academic, which today is the high school division.

Shattuck Military Academy of Faribault, Minnesota: the academy is now known as Shattuck St. Mary's School. Its archives were a valuable source of information about student life there. Mears' graduation address was reported in the school paper, *The Shattuck Cadet*, 1897.

schoolmate of Donald Stevens: Ralph Budd and R.C. Jamieson, "Frederick Mears," *Memoir* No. 968, American Society of Civil Engineers, 1939.

John Stevens at Marias Pass: This account draws from two sources, David McCullough's *Path Between the Seas* (Simon & Schuster, 1977), 461; and Eva Anderson's *Rails Across the Cascades* (World Publishing, 1987), 14-15.


## CHAPTER 2—Soldier and Engineer

Many of the particulars concerning Mears' duty in the Philippines came to light in a paper he wrote while attending the U.S. Staff College, entitled "The Spanish American War" (Mears' private collection).

"the Old Guard": Third Infantry of the U.S. Army, *The Old Guard* (Washington, D.C.: GPO, 1955). The Old Guard traces its lineage to the first American Regiment organized in 1784.

"The heat of the country was the poison of the islands": Agnes Newton Keith, *Bare Feet in the Palace* (Little, Brown, 1955) 157-61.

Fort Leavenworth: Built in 1827, it was a forerunner of the U.S. Army Command and General Staff College which Mears attended. More than 85,000 U.S. and international officers have passed through the Army's Senior Tactical College to become Leavenworth graduates.


## CHAPTER 3—Camelot in Panama

Four major sources proved especially useful in describing the construction of the Panama Canal, its history, and the engineers in

charge with whom Mears worked and established lasting friendships: David McCullough's *Path Between the Seas (Simon & Schuster,
1977)*, Joseph Bucklin Bishop and Farnham Bishop's *Goethals: Genius of the Panama Canal* (Harper & Row, 1930), John E. Minter's
*The Chagres: River of Westward Passage* (Rinehart, 1948), and Robert
Considine's *The Panama Canal* (Random House, 1951). I gathered
additional facts and statistics regarding this massive project when
I had the good fortune to visit the Panama Canal personally. Correspondence with Betty Mears-Meiggs about her childhood memories provided the colorful anecdotes from Mears' family life in the
Zone.

. . . "devil of mess": McCullough, *Path*, 462-463.

"I believe I face as discouraging. . . .": Bishop, *Genius*, 108.

"Big Smoke": Bishop, *Genius*, 133.

Mears' first assignment: Minter, *Chagres*, 368-369.

total excavation estimate: McCullough, *Path*, 529.

Stevens called to Washington: Considine, *Canal*, 95, 108-109.

Thirty-two miles would have to be moved, and Mears leads the
survey: Minter, *Chagres*, 356, 380-381.

John Barrett's observations of new Panama Railroad: Brown, "Man
Who Will Build," *New York Press*, 31 May 1914.

Roosevelt stunned and annoyed: McCullough, *Path*, 505.

Goethals appoints Mears to replace Budd: Bishop, *Goethals*, 207-211.

"I got an order. . .": Minter, *Chagres*, 364-365.

"I don't think you would make $7,500 a year": Considine, *Canal*, 129-130.

". . . no clouds on the horizon": Mears' summary of the work at Panama and his optimistic forecast appeared in a news story of 8 May 1911, entitled, "Big Canal Not Ready for Traffic Before '15," from Mears' personal file of clippings. (The San Francisco newspaper in which it appeared was not identified.) The implication is that he was visiting the Bay area, and presumably his mother and sister, at the time.

". . . one damn slide after another.": Minter, *Chagres*, 368-369.

"Few admirals then had as much tonnage under their command,": Brown, "Man Who Will Build," *New York Press*, 31 May 1914.

The moment lasted less than two minutes: McCullough, *Path*, 211.

"The lieutenant may conquer. . .": *Panama Morning Journal*, 2 May 1914.


## CHAPTER 4—The Intrigue of Alaska

Observations concerning conditions in Alaska prior to 1914, debate over its resources, and the Cordova coal party draw from Ernest Gruening's *The State of Alaska* (Random House, 1954). Background information about Franklin Lane and his policies appears in Anne Wintermute Lane and Louise Herrick Wall, *The Letters of Franklin K. Lane* (Houghton Mifflin, 1922).

observations about Upper Cook Inlet: William Healy Dall, *Alaska and Its Resources* (1870) reprint ed. (Lee & Ship, 1970).

Taft authorized to form railroad commission: Edwin M. Fitch, *The Alaska Railroad* (Praeger, 1967), 43-44.

"Who will control Alaska?": *Congressional Record*, 63d Cong., 2d sess., 1914, 51, pt. 2:1646.

background on Riggs and Edes: "Alaska Engineering Commission Appointed by President Wilson." *Engineering Record*, 69 (9 May 1914): 19.

President Wilson's leadership style: William Allen White, *Wilson the Man, His Times and His Task* (Houghton-Mifflin, 1924).

each bureau jealous of the other's authority: J. J. Underwood, "Alaska Fight to Throw Off Irons Backed," *Seattle Post Intelligencer*, 26 February 1922.

dispute over Mears' appointment: Ashmun Brown, "Tangle Grows out of Naming Alaska Board," *Seattle Post Intelligencer*, 6 May 1914; Edward B. Clark, "Secretary of Interior Lane Strikes Snag When He Orders Cavalry Officer to Yukon Without Asking Garrison," *Washington Post*, 12 May 1914.

Lane pushes joint resolution through Congress: S.J. Res. 145 "to provide for the detail of Lieut. Frederick Mears to perform service in connection with the building of the Alaskan Railway," *Statutes at Large* 38 (1914):772.

## CHAPTER 5—Preliminary Surveys, Afoot and Afloat

The complete account of the AEC survey work in Alaska was the prime source for the information in this chapter (House, *Reports of the Alaska Engineering Commission March 12, 1914-December 31, 1915*, 64th Congress, 1st sess., 1916, H. Doc. 610 part 2). In addition, Cliff Fuglestad, chief engineer for the Alaska Railroad, 1972-1979, offered his expert knowledge of the commission's 1914 investigations. He contributed valuable details concerning Mears' reconnaissance through Broad Pass and McPherson's remarkable efforts in the Kuskokwim area.

polite answers to reporters' questions: "Alaska Railroad Under Sole Control of President Wilson," *Oregon Daily Evening*, 30 May 1914.

conclusive evidence about the quality and quantity of coal: Dall, *Alaska and Its Resources*.

"I cannot tell you much. . .": "Work of Seattle Bureau is Lauded," *Seattle Post Intelligencer*, 2 June 1914.

Edes and Mears set up offices and hire laborers: "Surveying for Alaska System," *Railway and Marine News*, June 1914. An article in the *Pacific Builder and Engineer*, 30 May 1914, reported that the AEC opened its offices in Seattle's Alaska Building on May 23. Discussion of the commission's hiring practices appears in unidentified newspaper articles from May and June 1915, found in Mears' personal collection.

*Dirigo* at Knik: Bernadine La May Prince, *The Alaska Railroad* (Ken Wray, 1964), vol. 1:11.

AEC commissioners visit Juneau: one of the photographs in Mears' personal collection depicts a large contingent of AEC engineers and staff, all in coats and ties, posing together as a group on the dock at Juneau. The photograph is dated 10 June 1914.

"It is a credit to the AEC": Wilson, *Clouds*, 253.

"two little rail lines": Thomas Riggs, Jr., "The Government Railroad in Alaska: What Two Years and Limited Funds Have Accomplished," Engineering Record, 73, no. 19 (6 May 1916): 600-603.

choice of available harbors: Joshua Bernhardt, *The Alaska Engineering Commission: Its History, Activities and Organization* (Appleton, 1922), 13.

six people living in the area: "What Time Has Wrought," *Cook Inlet Pioneer*, 5 June 1915.

### CHAPTER 6—All Aboard for the Land of Promise

A valuable source for the information in this chapter and the next was the *Annual Report of the Chairman of the AEC to the Secretary of the Interior from February 1-December 31, 1915*, in *Reports of the Alaska Engineering Commission*, 64th Congress, 1st sess., 1916, H. Doc. 610 part 2, which documents the many activities the commission undertook during its first year in Alaska.

Alaska Syndicate: Harvey O'Conner, *The Guggenheims: The Making of an American Dynasty* (Covice-Friede, 1937).

John Ballaine's background and railroad building activities: Wilson, *Clouds*, 7; Clifford, *Rails North*, 69-70.

Guggenheims rebuff Ballaine: Wilson, *Clouds*, 15-16.

Lane's public announcement: "Alaska Route Chosen," *Washington Post*, 11 April 1915.

Ballaine's concerns about hiring practices: "Lane Says Work Will Be Done by Small Contractors," *Seward Gateway*, 12 April 1915.

Mears recruits in Canada: In a memo dated 9 April 1915, to Edes in Washington, Mears discusses his interview with and subsequent hiring of James O'Reilly from Winnipeg at a salary of $200 per month plus expenses. A note in the *Cook Inlet Pioneer*, 5 June 1915, also reports Canadian hires.

floating dock: Bernhardt, *Commission*, 22. Additional details about the temporary dock appear in Mears' report to Lane for that period, *Annual Report of the Chairman of the AEC to the Secretary of the Interior from February 1-December 31, 1915*, 64th Congress, 1st sess., 1916, H. Doc. 610 part 2, 185.

celebrations at Seward: "Wilson and Lane Cheered at the Moose Hall," *Seward Gateway*, 17 April 1915.

"Seward the Terminal": Another clipping from Mears' file is an article entitled "Big Sign for Dock," apparently from the *Seward Gateway*, 14 April 1915.

"Not a word will I say": "Mears Silent as a Sphinx," *Seward Gateway*, 26 April 1915.

"hell on wheels" and water for five cents a bucket: Wilson, *Clouds*, 101.

log hospital: daughter Betty had clear recollections of visiting the log hospital when her brother was born in December 1915. Photographs of the building appear in Prince, *Alaska Railroad*, vol. 1: 25, and in Evangeline Atwood's *Anchorage: Star of the North*.

notices posted around Tent Town: "Must Move Out," *Seward Gateway*, 1 May 1915.

prohibition of liquor: Report on Ship Creek Townsite from Mears to Lane, 2 June 1915, William Wilson collection for *Railroad in the Clouds*, Rasmuson Library, University of Alaska Fairbanks.

settlers demand action: Wilson, *Clouds*, 102.


## CHAPTER 7—From Wilderness to Town

In addition to the AEC's report to Lane covering this period, three other sources provided information about the beginnings of Anchorage: Wilson's *Railroad in the Clouds*, Carberry's *Patterns of the Past*, and issues of the *Cook Inlet Pioneer* from 1915-1916.

Christensen's arrival: Wilson, *Clouds*, 103.

"No one could walk on it without burning his boots": F.G. Carpenter, "Anchorage Boom City," *The Sunday Oregonian*, 30 April 1916.

record-setting auction: "Anchorage Lots Bring Big Prices at Auction Sale," *Cook Inlet Pioneer*, 17 July 1915.

"From personal observation . . .": The full text of Andrew Christensen's townsite auction speech was among the papers found in Mears' collection.

town plan a stock grid: Wilson, *Clouds*, 102.

white canvas sign: Carpenter, *Oregonian*, 30 April 1916.

Jeter's attempt to possess federal land: "Judge Brown's Decision in the T.H. Jeter Case," *Cook Inlet Pioneer*, 31 July 1915.

AEC funds for water tanks: Army Signal Corps telegram from Mears to Edes in Seward, 27 August 1915, William Wilson collection.

first school: Carberry, *Patterns*, 57.

decision over town name: letter from Mears to Edes in Seward, 8 October 1915, Alaska Railroad Headquarters files, National Archives Branch Depository, Seattle, Washington.

"I haven't any particular desire . . .": letter from Mears to Lane, 4 December 1915, Woodrow Wilson papers, Library of Congress.

"We've got to get along and scheme along": Wilson, *Clouds*, 140.

earnest approval: "Deficiency Appropriation for Alaskan Railroad," 64th Cong., 1st sess., 1915, H. Doc. 42.

## CHAPTER 8—Sidetracked by Skirmishes

Mears prepared extensive reports about station contracting, strikes, and the work along the Susitna River and on into Broad Pass and the Nenana Canyon. These served as the source for the majority of information in this chapter. They are compiled in *The Alaska Railroad, A General Review: 1914-1918* (Alaska Railroad headquarters files, National Archives Branch Depository, Seattle, Washington).

Congressional hearing dominated by Cannon: "Edes Had Facts and Figures," *Alaska Weekly Post*, 13 January 1916.

"Umph! It'll take so many cubic yards . . .": "Uncle Sam's Iron Men Open Up Alaska," *Seattle Sunday Times*, 30 January 1916.

$2 million awarded: *Alaska Railroad Record*, 1, no. 17 (6 March 1917): 129.

liquor problems persist and school enrollment doubles: Wilson, *Clouds*, 102, 106-107.

Land and Industrial Department established at Anchorage: *Alaska Railroad Record*, 1, no. 1 (14 November 1916): 4.

Alaska Federal Labor Union organized: Wilson, *Clouds*, 42-45.

"Every railroad in the country": memorandum from Mears to Edes requesting troops, 20 March 1916, William Wilson collection.

wages increased to 40 cents per hour: Wilson, *Clouds*, 43-44.

steady downpour: a photograph in Mears' private collection documents the heavy rain that fell when the commissioners went out in the longboat.

"Opposition will come . . .": letter from Edes to Lane, 17 August 1916, William Wilson collection.

$1,500 in the pot: Wilson, *Clouds*, 104.

3,700 men employed: letter from Mears to U.S. District Attorney, Third Judicial District, Valdez, Alaska, 16 September 1917. Alaska Railroad archives, University of Alaska Fairbanks.

Mears' interview at Seward: "Surprising Delay of U.S. Railroad," *Alaska Weekly Post*, 1 December 1916.

accusations of intentional delays: *Fairbanks Garden Island Citizen*, 10 December 1916.

success means more than salary: Thomas Riggs Jr., "Fairbanks Newspaper Is Making Show of Ignorance," *Nenana News*, 23 December 1916.

Mears travels to Washington, D.C. in December 1916: On his way east, Mears reportedly stopped in Portland to see his brother and in San Francisco to see his mother. "Captain Mears Here," *Morning Oregonian*, 4 December 1916.

## CHAPTER 9—Tranquility at Home, Turmoil Abroad

For material in this chapter concerning coal mining and port facilities, I relied most heavily on Bernhardt's *The Alaska Engineering Commission, Its History, Activities, and Organization*, and on L. J. Campbell's "Alaska's Coal" published as a supplement to *Alaska's Railroads: Alaska Geographic* 19, no. 4 (1992): 81-91.

Delaney remembers Mears: Wilson, *Clouds*, 139.

best equipped hospital: Prince, *Alaska Railroad*, vol.1: 162-163.

"They are going to have decent treatment!": J.M. Aldrich, "Ranks Alaska Railway Next to Panama Canal," *Washington Evening Star*, 9 February 1922.

"Nothing was spared . . .": Carberry, *Patterns*, 25; personal communication with Cappy Faroe, 1978.

recuperation from pneumonia: *Alaska Railroad Record*, 1, no. 22 (10 April 1917): 169.

coal's importance to war effort: Francis S. Peabody, "Alaska's Coal Vital Factor," *Seward Gateway*, 9 July 1917.

Gerig hired: *Alaska Railroad Record*, 1, no.18 (13 March 1917): 141. Gerig had worked for the Isthmian Canal Commission at Cristobal and Gatun in Panama, 1905-1908.

Navy secretary petitions Lane: letter from Josephus Daniels to Franklin Lane, 12 March 1917. Frederick Mears archive collection, Rasmuson Library, University of Alaska Fairbanks.

". . . not about to risk my reputation": letter from Edes to Lane, 16 August 1916, William Wilson collection.

dredge operation: *Alaska Railroad Record*, 1, no. 30 (12 June 1917): 233.

early closing of port: letter from Mears to Edes, 26 November 1917. Mears records, Military Reference Branch, National Archives, Washington, D.C.

"I am not thinking of the loss of property . . .": Eugene Barker, W. Dodd, and H.S. Commager, *Our Nation's Development* (Row Peterson & Co., 1934), 507.

"Feudalism is making its last stand . . .": Franklin Lane, "Why Do We Fight Germany," *Congressional Record*, 8 June 1917.

## CHAPTER 10—Off to War

George M. Studley's *History of the 31ˢᵗ Railway Regiment* (1941) provided valuable details for this chapter. It describes the formation of the 31ˢᵗ unit at Fort Leavenworth, recounts its subsequent activities in France, and documents Mears' promotions under General Atterbury. John Westwood's *Railways at War* (Howell North, 1980) devotes a chapter to the work of the U.S. Transportation Corps in World War I.

Mears ordered to recruit: "Colonel Mears Will Raise Railroad Regiment," *Alaska Railroad Record*, 2, no.8 (1 January 1918): 57-63.

farewell celebration: "Farewell Given Major and Mrs. Mears," *Anchorage Daily Times*, 3 January 1918.

farewell speeches: "Andrew Christensen Praised Mears," *Alaska Railroad Record*, 2, no.9: 68, in Prince, *Alaska Railroad* vol. 1.

"Mears seemed more interested in enjoying his children,": *Seward Gateway*, 8 January 1918.

"You would think . . .": Letter from Christensen to Edes, 14 January 1918, William Wilson collection.

Mears commissioned colonel in command of 31ˢᵗ Railway Engineers: *Alaska Railroad Record*, 12 January 1918, in Prince, vol. 1: 221.

"I wish you to know . . .": Letter from Lane to Mears, 26 January 1918. Mears papers, Military Reference Branch, National Archives.

narrow gauge French railroads: "The Dinky Lines' World War I Origins," *Locomotive and Railway Preservation*, May-June 1989.

"Atta boy . . .": Jack Lincke, "Building Roads But Incident in Commission's Many Duties," *Anchorage Daily Times*, 3 February 1921.

## CHAPTER 11—Entrusted with Full Command

Specifics about the Hallowell delegation to Alaska derive from an account in the 14 August 1919 *Seattle Daily Times* and from Betty's recollections.

Edes driving the last spike: *Alaska Railroad Record*, 17 September 1918, in Prince, vol. 1: 247.

Wickersham on coal: *Congressional Record*, 65th Cong., 3d sess., 1919, 57:3706-3708.

more interested in handling their own business: Wilson, *Clouds*, 124.

Ralph Budd, Mears' contemporary and fellow engineer in Panama, would make his mark in 1932 by pioneering the use of diesel engines for passenger trains. The first high speed, stainless steel train was called the Pioneer Zephyr.

steaming test of bituminous coal: Wilson, *Clouds*, 14.

Lane had every confidence in Mears: Letter from Hallowell to Jane Mears, 17 November 1919, Mears' private collection.

railroad built "entirely without graft": Report from Lane to President Wilson, Lane and Wall, *Letters*, 260.

Lane shelves idea of Alaska board and prepares to resign: Lane and Wall, *Letters*, 322-360.

## CHAPTER 12—Equal to the Task

William Wilson's painstaking research provided many colorful details about the commission's activities in 1919-1920. These are interspersed throughout his book, *Railroad in the Clouds*. Specific to this chapter are the post-war reorganization of the AEC, Ballaine's interview with Lane, background information about James Wickersham, the failure of Browne's bridge at Tanana, Secretary Payne's inspection trip, and the incorporation of Anchorage.

first bridges built of heavy timbers: Prince, *Alaska Railroad*, vol. 1: 202-203.

loop trestle experience and AEC's early river operations: Clifford, *Rails North*, 85, 96.

"In my mind, to require excessive clearance . . .": Letter from Mears to Payne, 6 May 1920, Mears files, Military Reference Branch, National Archives.

"Round up those men . . .": Cable from Mears to Marshal Brenneman, Valdez, Alaska, 12 May 1920.

$5,000 refunded after flu epidemic: "AEC To Be Reimbursed for Expenditures Attached Care of Natives During Epidemic," *Anchorage Daily Times*, 3 February 1921.

Payne and Daniels visit Alaska: a photograph of the two men at Mile 243, the end of steel in July 1920, appears in Cohen's pictorial history, *Rails Across the Tundra*, 38.

no evidence to validate the charges: Wilson, *Clouds*, 138.

official transfer to Army Corps of Engineers: Mears' private papers include the document bearing Jonathan Wainwright's signature.

they had a good thing in federal paternalism: William H. Wilson, "The Founding of Anchorage: Federal Townbuilding on the Last Frontier," *Pacific Northwest Quarterly*, July 1967, 131-141.

Barndollar's remarks urging incorporation: "New Law Extends to Towns Along Railroad," *Alaska Railroad Record*, 3, no. 28: 222.

## CHAPTER 13—Spans of Steel, Will of Iron

In the writings of Jack Lincke, a reporter for the *Anchorage Daily Times*, I found an unexpected treasure. Lincke's first-hand accounts of working conditions "on the line" paint vivid pictures of men, horses, and locomotives forging ahead with construction operations in the dead of winter. Lincke's series of articles includes "Out Along the Firing Line with Colonel Mears and His Doughboys," 24 January 1921, and "Home of the Storm King Invaded as Railroad Moves North," 26 January 1921.

"It is necessary to stretch the imagination . . .": Frederick Mears, *General Review of the Alaska Railroad*, Press of the Alaska Railroad, 1918.

concrete piers built at Susitna River crossing: "Great Alaskan Bridge Built during Coldest Weather," *Railway Age*, 71, no.3: 103-105.

"Satisfactory arrangements were made . . .": E. M. Braford's letter appeared in the *Fairbanks Weekly*, 17 December 1920.

work by American Bridge Co.: E.G. Amesbury, "Erection of Hurricane Gulch Bridge in Alaska," *Engineering News Record*, 8, no.4 (26 January 1922). The author was assistant chief engineer of the erecting department for the Pittsburgh, Pennsylvania, company.

## CHAPTER 14—A Fight to the Finish

Discussion of the Teapot Dome scandal and Albert Fall's tenure with the Harding administration draws from Bert Noggle's *Teapot Dome: Oil and Politics in the 1920s* (Louisiana State Universiy Press, 1962). A complete summary account of correspondence and testimony related to the issue of Mears' salary payments appears in U.S. House Committee on the Territories, *Report Authorizing the Reappointment of Frederick Mears as a Commissioned Officer of the Regular Army (to accompany H.J. Res. 316)*, 67th Cong., 1st sess., 1922, H. Doc. 955.

". . . if the whole thing were scrapped": House Committee on the Territories, *Hearings on H.R. 226*, 68th Cong., 1st sess., 1924, 4111.

Payne's request for salary raise: "Criticism Made of Alaska Road," *Seattle Post Intelligencer*, 9 January 1921.

"Military men do not know money": *Congressional Record*, 66th Cong., 3d sess., December 1920-January 1921, vol. 60, pt. 1: 1009-1012.

"If building roads was all there was . . .": Jack Lincke, "Building Railroad But Incident in Commission's Many Duties," *Anchorage Daily Times*, 3 February 1921.

Burton Barndollar's assurances to Mears about pay: Memorandum from Barndollar to Mears, 28 April 1921, Alaska Railroad Headquarters File, National Archives Branch Depository, Seattle, Washington.

Ballaine claims he'll replace Mears: *Seattle Daily Times*, 14 March 1921.

Fairbanks Commercial Club supports Mears: Letter to Secretary Fall, 14 March 1921, Alaska Railroad archives, University of Alaska Fairbanks.

Mears' publicity tour: "Alaska Road Pushed, Chairman Tells of Progress," *Seattle Daily Times*, 6 February 1921.

"Alaska, long the lure . . .": "Alaska to Play Big Role in Affairs of America, Avers Chief of Rail Work," *Sunday Oregonian*, 6 February 1921.

Alaska Railroad compared to other railroads in the west: Frederick Mears, "Alaska Railroad," a speech presented 20 January 1921, and reprinted in *Journal of the Western Society of Engineers*, 26, no. 9 (September 1921): 323-325.

"It was not intended or expected . . .": Wilson, *Clouds*, 146.

"In justice to the Alaska Syndicate . . .": Memo from Edes to Lane, 15 May 1919. Alaska Railroad archives, University of Alaska Fairbanks.

"Before additional conclusions . . .": Letter from Mears to Bone, 14 June 1922. Alaska Railroad archives, University of Alaska Fairbanks.

Ballaine's theory about the railroad and the syndicate: "How Neglected Alaska is Being Throttled," *Dearborn Independent*, 18 March 1922.

Racquet Club dinner: a menu and list of guests from the 18 March 1922, event was among Mears' mementos. The eight-course, all-Alaskan repast included reindeer meat, Chinook salmon, Fairbanks potatoes, and Sitka fruits.

Mears reinstated by joint resolution: *Statutes at Large* 42 (1922): 831.

Eklutna hydroelectric project: letter from Mears to Fall, 27 September 1922. AGO Files, Military Reference Branch, National Archives.

railroad to serve military needs: speech by Colonel Mears to Anchorage Chamber of Commerce, records of the Alaska Railroad, State of Alaska archives, Juneau.

Tanana bridge considered more dramatic: Wilson, *Clouds*, 82.


## CHAPTER 15—The Golden Spike

Many accounts of the golden spike ceremony have been published over the years. I chose to rely on Wilson's in *Clouds*, and on Clifford's in *Rails North*. The full texts of Work's and Harding's speeches were among the mementos in Mears' file.

"The purser of the *Alameda* . . .": letter from Governor Bone to Mayor Conroy, 19 July 1923. State of Alaska archives, Juneau.

". . . beyond the dreams of Croesus': Noggle, *Teapot Dome*, 37-51.

LaFollette on Fall, "It would have been possible. . .": *Wall Street Journal*, 14 April 1922.

"The Strangling of the Alaska Railroad": A copy of Ballaine's tract is included in the report from the House Committee on the Territories, *Hearings on H.R. 226*, 68th Cong., 1st sess., 1924.

U.S. Department of Commerce optimistic findings: J. F. Keeley, "A Hundred Million Stockholders Own Railroad Opening Up Alaska." This was another clipping found in Mears' collection. The approximate date is February 1922. Keeley was assistant chief of transportation for the U.S. Department of Commerce at the time he wrote it.

"voyage of understanding": Noggle, *Teapot Dome*.

what the railroad needed was a promoter: J. J. Underwood, "Problem of Operation to Be Studied." This article from an unidentified Juneau newspaper (May? 1921) was in Mears' file of clippings.

Fall resigns: "Secretary Fall to Quit Cabinet." *New York Times*, 3 January 1923.

"an attitude of dignity . . .": "Anchorage to Pay Homage to Col. F. Mears at Public Reception Tonight," *Anchorage Daily Times*, 4 May 1923.

Ballaine's allegations of "contagion": Grafton Wilcox, "President Is Told of Plots to Gain Graft," *San Francisco Chronicle*, 16 July 1923.

"for the greater personal recognition . . .": Grafton Wilcox, "Harding Hears Big Alaskan Row," *Morning Oregonian*, 16 July 1923.

"the word bribery had not been used . . .": "Trouble in Alaska," *San Francisco Chronicle*, 16 July 1923.

". . . an illness that was part terror . . .": William A. White quoted in Noggle, *Teapot Dome*, 58.

Ballaine's obituary: *Anchorage Times*, 15 January 1941.

"a matter of politics": U.S. House Committee on the Territories, *Relief of Special Disbursing Agents of the Alaska Engineering Commission: Hearings on H.R. 226*, 68th Cong., 1st sess., 1924, 51-55.

golden spike returned to Mears: From a St. Paul newspaper clipping, "Explains Work of Clubs in Alaska," 18 September 1923. The article states that Jane Mears exhibited the golden spike when she gave an address about Alaska to the Women's Welfare League.

## CHAPTER 16—Once an Engineer, Always an Engineer

The details of Mears' later career came primarily from his daughter Betty, and from Ralph Budd and R. C. Jamieson, "Frederick Mears," *Memoir* No. 968, American Society of Civil Engineers, 1939.

General Pershing's wishes on Mears' retirement: Letter from Pershing to Mears dated 13 July 1923.

Cascade tunnel: a thorough explanation of the design and construction of the tunnel appears in an article Mears wrote for *Railway and Marine News*, entitled "Conquering the Cascades" (January 1929). Eva Anderson's *Rails Across the Cascades* (1952) gives colorful stories and details about the work behind completion of the tunnel.

national broadcast for Cascade tunnel dedication: a program from the 12 January 1929 dedication ceremony was among Mears' mementos. It describes how celebrants participated live from radio stations across the country.

Cedaroc: In 1990 I had the good fortune to interview Mary Grace Galvin, who was a close neighbor of the Mears family during their summers at Cedaroc.

"As an engineer and executive . . .": Budd and Jamieson, *Memoir*, 5.

Frederick Mears III's book *Carrier Combat* (Ballantine, 1944) was accepted for publication before he died.

"footprints" of Fort Mears: D. Colt Denfeld, *The Defense of Dutch Harbor* (Anchorage, AK: Alaska District, U.S. Corps of Engineers, 1987).

Governor Bone on captains of industry: "Dawn of a New Day for Alaska," *Business Chronicle of the Pacific Northwest*, 12, no. 20 (8 April 1922).

# ACKNOWLEDGMENTS

A spirited discussion with fellow board members of Historic Anchorage, Inc., prompted my decision to write the life story of Frederick Mears. I sincerely appreciate the support and encouragement I received from Elizabeth Guess, Diane Hayes, and Kay Linton, who persuaded me to proceed.

My research inevitably led me to question why Colonel Mears' official papers and documents had remained unstudied and had never received public attention. I found a partial explanation in that the quiet, reserved man never sought the limelight. He took satisfaction in knowing that the quality of the work he completed would speak for itself. Until the time of her own death at age eighty-two, Mears' daughter Betty shared with me many such aspects of her father's personality. I am grateful for having known her.

When Mears' granddaughter Marilyn Richards first learned of my interest in writing a book about her distinguished relative, she and Betty willingly entrusted me with his private papers. Through the gracious support of these women, I also received permission to access Mears' records housed at the National Archives in Washington, D.C., and at the U.S. Military History Institute in Carlisle Barracks, Pennsylvania. In addition, historian William H. Wilson was most generous in granting me permission to use material from his book *Railroad in the Clouds: The Alaska Railroad in the Age of Steam 1914-1945*.

Because of the intensive research required for a book of this nature, I relied heavily upon the experience and generosity of many archivists and librarians, who helped locate sources and facts necessary for completion of the manuscript. Credit is due them for contributing to the body of knowledge about Colonel Frederick

Mears, but I alone am responsible for any shortcomings the book
may contain. Among the individuals who assisted me, particularly
deserving of thanks are M. Diane Brenner, archivist for the Anchorage Museum of History and Art; Karen Morrissey of the Alaska
Railroad Corporation in Anchorage, who gave me permission to
research the Alaska Railroad record collection at the National Archives Sand Point (Washington) Branch, and archivist Joyce Justice
there; Bruce Merrill, director of the Alaska Collection at the Loussac
Library in Anchorage; Elizabeth Morriset, director of the Alaska
Collection at Alaska Pacific University; and Brian Hawkins director
of interlibrary-loan services at UAA-APU Consoritum Library in
Anchorage. Elsewhere in the state, Patricia Linville and Tim
Sczawinski of the Seward Community Library were most helpful,
as were Marilee Koszewski and Ann Landkammer of Seward; archivists Ron Inouye and Diane Kokborg of the Rasmuson Library,
and Pam Odom of the University of Alaska Press in Fairbanks;
and State of Alaska librarian Kathryn Shelton and archivists Karen
Crane, Lawrence Hibpshman, and Al Minnick in Juneau. In Sitka,
Evelyn Bonner and the staff of the Stratton Library at Sheldon
Jackson College, and the staff of the Kettleson Library facilitated
my inter-library loan requests.

Through correspondence with H. L. Anderton, a personal
friend from Arlington, Virginia, I obtained valuable information
about Mears' executive confrontations that greatly enhanced the
credibility of the manuscript. I wish to express my thanks for the
assistance I was given by the following people on my visit to the
nation's capital: the staff of Alaska Senator Ted Stevens, John
Slonaker at the Library of Congress, and Joan Williamson and William Lind at the Military Reference Branch of the National Archives. At the U. S. Military Institute Richard Sommers and Colonel
Donald Shaw were especially helpful. My thanks also go to the ar-
chival staffs at the Minnesota Historical Society Library and at the
Suzzalo Library, University of Washington; to Nancy Gale Compau
at the Spokane Public Library; to Fr. Neill Meany at the Crosby
Library, Gonzaga Preparatory School; to Mildred Marple at Shattuck

Preparatory School; and to Lesley Hendricks of the Seminole, Florida, Panama Canal Museum.

Several individuals granted interviews that added a human touch to my findings. Of those interviewed, I'm especially grateful to Bert Wennerstrom, who worked for the Alaska Railroad as a young man and was often a dinner guest at the Mears home; Anchorage pioneer school teacher Selma Smith; and Mary Grace Galvin, once a close friend and neighbor of the Mears family at Glacier Park.

I want to extend special thanks to Cliff Fuglestad of Anchorage, who was chief engineer of the Alaska Railroad from 1972 to 1979. He offered an excellent critique of the manuscript relative to early survey work and construction problems. Edward Lynch of Vancouver, Washington, provided important technical information from his personal library about early railroad construction. William Steward of Spokane, sent pertinent information relative to the Cascade Tunnel; Barbara Tornquist supplied leads about the St. Paul Union Depot; and Jim and Millie Tapscott of Wasilla, Alaska, were kind enough to lend me rare memorabilia from the early days of the railroad.

I greatly appreciate the effort and care others gave to reviewing the manuscript in various stages: Davis Carson of Tulsa, Harriet LaMair of Denver, Elizabeth Palacios of Santa Fe, William Platt of Sea Ranch, California, and editor-publisher Robert Woolsey, of Sitka. Professor Jane Evanson, author of *Breaking into Print*, generously gave of her time, attention, and enthusiasm to see the book through to publication. In particular I want to thank LuAnne Dowling, my editor in Anchorage, whose sensitive and professional help enabled me to stay the course through the many months of our collaboration.

Finally, I am deeply indebted to my husband, Ed, and to our family for their support during the research and the writing of the manuscript. They were my constant companions and bulwark throughout this long literary journey.

# SELECT BIBLIOGRAPHY

## BOOKS

Atwood, Evangeline. *Anchorage: All-America City*. Portland, OR: Binfords & Mort, 1957.

_____. *Anchorage: Star of the North*. Tulsa, OK: Continental Heritage Press, 1982.

Barker, Eugene, W. Dodd, and H.S. Commager. *Our Nation's Development*. Evanston IL: Row Peterson & Co., 1934.

Bernhardt, Joshua. *The Alaska Engineering Commission, Its History, Activities and Organization*. New York: D. Appleton, 1922.

Bishop, Joseph Bucklin, and Farnham Bishop. *Goethals: Genius of the Panama Canal*. New York: Harper & Row, 1930.

Burch, Franklin Ward. "Alaska's Railroad Frontier: Railroads and Federal Development Policy, 1898-1915." Dissertation, Catholic University of America, 1965.

Campbell, L. J. "Alaska's Coal." *Alaska Geographic*, 19, no. 4 (1992): 81-91.

Carberry, Michael J. *Patterns of the Past: Inventory of Anchorage's Heritage Resources*. Anchorage, AK: Municipality of Anchorage, 1979.

Clifford, Howard. *Rails North*. Seattle, WA: Superior Publishing, 1981.

Cohen, Stan. *Rails Across the Tundra*. Missoula, MT: Pictorial Histories Publishing Co., 1984.

Considine, Robert. *The Panama Canal*. New York: Random House, 1951.

Dall, William Healy. *Alaska and Its Resources* (1870). Reprint ed. Boston: Lee & Ship, 1970.

Denfeld, D. Colt. *The Defense of Dutch Harbor, Alaska, from Military Construction to Base Clean-Up.* Anchorage, AK: Alaska District, U.S. Corps of Engineers, 1987.

Fitch, Edwin M. *The Alaska Railroad.* New York: Praeger, 1967.

Gruening, Ernest. *The State of Alaska.* New York: Random House, 1954.

Holbrook, Stewart H. *James J. Hill.* Great Lives in Brief series. New York: Alfred A. Knopf, 1967.

Keith, Agnes Newton. *Bare Feet in the Palace.* Boston: Little, Brown & Co., 1955.

Lane, Anne W., and Louise H. Wall. *The Letters of Franklin Lane.* Boston: Houghton Mifflin, 1922.

McCullough, David. *Path Between the Seas: The Creation of the Panama Canal 1870-1914.* New York: Simon & Schuster, 1977.

Mears, Frederick III. *Carrier Combat.* New York: Ballantine, 1944.

Minter, J.E. *The Chagres: River of the Westward Passage.* New York: Rinehart, 1948.

Naske, Claus M., and Herman E. Slotnick, *Alaska: A History of the 49th State,* 2d ed. Norman, OK: University of Oklahoma Press, 1987.

Noggle, Bert. *Teapot Dome: Oil and Politics in the 1920s.* Baton Rouge, LA: Louisiana State University Press, 1962.

O'Conner, Harvey. *The Guggenheims: The Making of an American Dynasty.* New York: Covice-Friede, 1937.

Prince, Bernadine LaMay. *The Alaska Railroad.* 2 vols. Anchorage, AK: Ken Wray Printing, 1964.

Russell, Francis. *The Shadow of Blooming Grove: Warren Harding in His Times.* New York: McGraw-Hill, 1968.

Sinclair, Andrew. *The Available Man: The Life Behind the Mask of Warren Gamaliel Harding.* New York: Macmillan, 1965.

Stegner, Wallace. *Angle of Repose*. Garden City, NY: Doubleday, 1971.

Studley, George M. *History of the 31ˢᵗ Railway Regiment*. Berkeley, CA: Veterans of the 31ˢᵗ Railway Engineers, 1941.

Wellman, Paul I. *Death on the Prairie: The Thirty Years' Struggle for the Western Plains*. Lincoln, NE: University of Nebraska Press, 1934.

Westwood, John. *Railways at War*. San Diego, CA: Howell North Books, 1980.

White, William Allen. *Wilson the Man, His Times and His Task*. Boston: Houghton-Mifflin, 1924.

Wilgus, William J. *Transporting the A.E.F. in Western Europe 1917-1919*. New York: Columbia University Press, 1931.

Wilson, William H. *Railroad in the Clouds: The Alaska Railroad in the Age of Steam, 1914-1945*. Boulder, CO: Pruett Publishing, 1977.

## BOOKLETS AND MONOGRAPHS

Anderson, Eva. *Rails Across the Cascades*, 4th ed. Wenatchee, Washington: World Publishing, 1987.

Budd, Ralph, and R.C. Jamieson. "Frederick Mears." *Memoirs*. American Society of Civil Engineers Memoir No. 968. 1939.

Chance, David H. *Sentinel of Silence: A Brief History of Fort Spokane*. Pacific Northwest National Parks Association, 1981.

*Dedication and Opening of the Cascade Tunnel*. Great Northern Railway. 12 January 1929.

Greguras, Fred M. *The History of the Post of Omaha, Fort Omaha, Fort Crook, and the Quartermaster Depots*. Omaha, NE: Command and Support Center, 1977.

Page, Charles, and Frank Meacham. *Description of Military Posts*. Omaha, NE: Douglas County Historical Society, n.d.

Rose, Mary. *Vancouver's Historic Officers Row*. Vancouver, WA: City of Vancouver, n.d.

*A Self-Guided Tour of Fort Leavenworth, the Gateway to the West*. Fort Leavenworth, KS: Fort Leavenworth Historical Society, 1981.

Small, Charles S. *Rails to the Diggings: Construction Railroads of the Panama Canal*. Railroad Monographs, 1981.

The Third Infantry of the U.S. Army. *The Old Guard: History of the Third Infantry*.Washington D.C.: GPO, 1955.

# INDEX